Great Games for Big Activity Balls

Todd Strong, MSc, MEd
and
Bernie DeKoven, MA

Human Kinetics

Library of Congress Cataloging-in-Publication Data

Strong, Todd.
  Great games for big activity balls / Todd Strong, Bernie DeKoven.
    p. cm.
  ISBN-13: 978-0-7360-7481-0 (soft cover)
  ISBN-10: 0-7360-7481-3 (soft cover)
  1. Ball games 2. Balls (Sporting goods) 3. Games. I. DeKoven, Bernie, 1941- II. Title.
  GV861.S87 2009
  796.3--dc22

                                      2009028724

ISBN-10: 0-7360-7481-3 (print)
ISBN-13: 978-0-7360-7481-0 (print)

The Web addresses cited in this text were current as of August 2009, unless otherwise noted.

Acquisitions Editor: Gayle Kassing, PhD; **Developmental Editor:** Amy Stahl; **Assistant Editors:** Anne Rumery and Lauren Morenz; **Copyeditor:** Joy Wotherspoon; **Graphic Designer:** Joe Buck; **Graphic Artist:** Denise Lowry; **Cover Designer:** Keith Blomberg; **Photographer (cover):** Wilmer Zehr; **Photographer (interior):** David duChemin, unless otherwise noted; photo on page 26 courtesy of Todd Strong; photo of Bernie DeKoven on page 225 courtesy of Bernie DeKoven; **Photo Production Manager:** Jason Allen; **Art Manager:** Kelly Hendren; **Associate Art Manager:** Alan L. Wilborn; **Illustrator:** Alan L. Wilborn; **Printer:** Versa Press

Printed in the United States of America   10 9 8 7 6 5 4 3 2 1

The paper in this book is certified under a sustainable forestry program.

Human Kinetics
Web site: www.HumanKinetics.com

United States: Human Kinetics, P.O. Box 5076, Champaign, IL 61825-5076
800-747-4457
e-mail: humank@hkusa.com

Canada: Human Kinetics, 475 Devonshire Road Unit 100, Windsor, ON N8Y 2L5
800-465-7301 (in Canada only)
e-mail: info@hkcanada.com

Europe: Human Kinetics, 107 Bradford Road, Stanningley, Leeds LS28 6AT, United Kingdom
+44 (0) 113 255 5665
e-mail: hk@hkeurope.com

Australia: Human Kinetics, 57A Price Avenue, Lower Mitcham, South Australia 5062
08 8372 0999
e-mail: info@hkaustralia.com

New Zealand: Human Kinetics, P.O. Box 80, Torrens Park, SA, 5062
0800 222 062
e-mail: info@hknewzealand.com

E4489

Contents

• • • • • • • • • • • • • •

Game Finder v • Preface xii • Acknowledgments xiv

Part I   Learning About Big Activity Balls 1

1   Big Activity Ball Games: Huge Benefits, Huge Fun 3

2   The Nuts and Bolts of Using a Big Activity Ball 19

Part II   Learning the Games 33

3   Big Cooperative Games: Activities Designed for Big Play 35

4   Super Sports: Traditional Games Played in a Big Way 79

5   Humongous Playground Games: Large-Scale Versions of Favorite Childhood Activities 115

6   Big Athletic Games: Large Track-and-Field Events . . . 135

7   Ginormous World-Record Challenges: Using Your Big Activity Ball to Earn a Place in History 155

8   Very Big Midways: Giant Carnival Games 173

9   Making a Big Splash: Playing Water Games With a Big Activity Ball 203

About the Authors 225

Game Finder

As players grow up, they develop physical, emotional, and cognitive skills. Although fun is the main goal of the games in this book, play can also be an important part of the maturation process. Playing with a big activity ball in a social setting helps children interact with peers and adults in new ways. Each game description in part II highlights the skills that particular activity develops. The skills are fully explained here, broken down into four large categories: social skills, personal behaviors, perceptual and physical skills, and basic motor skills.

Social Skills

Games with a big activity ball almost always happen in a social setting. As such, most of the games in this book help develop social skills, such as cooperation, trust, problem solving, communication, appropriate touch, and adaptability.

- **Cooperation:** Playing with a big activity ball promotes cooperation among the participants. Players must work together to control such a large ball.

- **Trust:** Players must have a certain amount of trust in their teammates. This can be physical trust to not let other players fall to the ground or emotional trust to allow players to let each other be a little whimsical without negative judgments. In most cases the term *trust* used here is the physical kind, knowing that players will take turns acting as spotters.

- **Problem solving:** A lot of the games allow for multiple approaches to achieve similar results. Problem solving puts an emphasis on players taking an active role in how they will proceed in the game, not just following a well-defined set of prescribed rules.

- **Communication:** Games that emphasize communication empower players to speak with and listen to one another.

- **Appropriate touch:** Players come in contact with the big activity ball in every game, but they may also need to know how to control their physical contact with other players, both teammates and opposing players.
- **Adaptability:** Players may need to adapt their behavior to fit in with other players or accommodate the rules of the game.

Personal Behavior

Even when players are fully involved in a group game, they must still act as both teammates and individuals. The types of personal behavior considered here are self-control, creativity, and improvisational acting.

- **Self-control:** As much fun as these games are, players need to remember that there are other people around them. Behavior, both physical and emotional, should not be so exuberant that a player's actions intimidate other players.
- **Creativity:** In these games, players incorporate their own original ideas and imagination into the games.
- **Improvisational acting:** In these games the players take advantage of a simple outline of an idea and spontaneously develop the idea into their short-term fantasy.

Perceptual and Physical Skills

Games and sports are an excellent way for children of all ages to get instant feedback on their physical developmental skills. The perceptual and physical skills here include: keen vision, coordination, rapid response, strength, and endurance.

- **Keen vision:** Given the context of games with big activity balls, it may seem a bit silly to talk about keen vision. With that caveat, these games involve some amount of visual acuity.
- **Coordination:** Some games require complex body movements, either at the same time or in quick succession. Another way to think about this is to see if players can rub and pat a big activity ball at the same time.

- **Rapid response:** The ability to react quickly is an important component of these games.
- **Strength:** These games reward those who can demonstrate physical power and energy.
- **Endurance:** In these games players must sustain their efforts for a prolonged length of time.

Basic Motor Skills

Sports and many games are physical. That's no less true when engaging in big versions of these activities. The basic motor skills used to play these games include walking, running, balancing, and throwing and catching.

- **Walking:** These games involve moving from one place to another at a fairly slow pace.
- **Running:** These games also involve moving around but at a slightly faster pace.
- **Balancing:** These games utilize a combination of proprioceptor stimuli and appropriate muscle response.
- **Throwing and catching:** A big activity ball is pretty big for one player to throw or catch. The instances of throwing and catching refer to smaller, foam balls.

Key

We packed this book with as many good games as we could think of. The game finder is our attempt to make the games more accessible than by just the chapter divisions in the book. One way to use the game finder is as an alphabetical list of games. Rather than try to remember which chapter a particular game is in, just look up the game alphabetically in the game finder, and you can find what page the game is on.

You can also search for games according to the various skills listed in the skills columns by looking for a game that may develop or reinforce a particular skill. Find the appropriate skill column, and scan down until you find what skill you are looking for. Look across that row to the left, and you may have found an excellent game for your situation.

** = Primary skill
* = Secondary skill

Game	Page number	Social skills	Personal behavior skills	Perceptual and physical skills	Basic motor skills
100-Meter Roll	136	Cooperation*			Running**
Airmail	60			Strength** Keen vision*	Throwing and catching**
Ball Crawl	49	Trust**		Coordination** Rapid response*	
Ball Surfing	73	Trust**	Self-control*		
Big Baseball	96	Cooperation**			Running*
Big Billiards	80	Cooperation*			Throwing and catching**
Big Bocce	83			Strength** Keen vision*	
Big Bouncer	196	Trust (leaners)*		Strength (bouncers)** Coordination (bouncers)*	Balancing (leaners)**
Big Double Basketball	86	Cooperation*			Walking** Running**
Big Kid Pile-Up	163	Cooperation** Problem solving*			Balancing**
Big Volley	100	Cooperation**		Coordination** Keen vision*	
Boulder Roll	40	Cooperation**		Coordination** Keen vision*	Running**
Bounce Rope	129	Cooperation**		Rapid response*	Throwing and catching**
Bounce Scotch	126	Cooperation** Problem solving* Communication*		Coordination**	
Broad Bounce	146			Strength**	Throwing and catching*
Bumper Ball	75	Trust**	Self-control*	Strength**	
Colossal Bowling	102	Cooperation*		Strength**	
Colossal Cricket	88			Rapid response** Strength*	Running**
Crab Soccer	94			Rapid response** Coordination** Endurance*	

Game	Page number	Social skills	Personal behavior skills	Perceptual and physical skills	Basic motor skills
Donut Rolls	38	Cooperation*		Coordination** Rapid response** Keen vision*	
Eclipse	63	Cooperation**		Coordination* Rapid response*	Throwing and catching**
Eight Square	121			Coordination** Rapid response** Keen vision*	
Extreme Jacks	118	Cooperation**		Rapid response** Coordination*	
Flip Your Giant Lid	124			Rapid response*	Throwing and catching**
Giant Shooting Gallery	192			Keen vision** Coordination*	Throwing and catching**
Gigantic Miniature Golf	104			Strength** Keen vision*	
Ginormous Juggling	159	Cooperation**		Strength** Endurance*	
Great Wall Handball	112			Coordination** Rapid response*	
Group Ball Touch	161	Cooperation** Appropriate touch** Problem solving*			
Group Dribbling	46	Cooperation** Problem solving*		Coordination** Keen vision*	Walking* Running*
Group Stretches	52	Trust**	Self-control*	Strength**	
Hair Dryer	77		Creativity** Improvisational acting*		
High Throw	143			Strength** Coordination*	
Hip Check	36	Cooperation**	Self-control*	Strength**	
Honkin' Big Discus	150			Strength** Coordination*	
Hoop on the Ball (Giant Ring Toss)	186			Coordination** Keen vision*	

(continued)

Game Finder *(continued)*

Game	Page number	Social skills	Personal behavior skills	Perceptual and physical skills	Basic motor skills
Humongous Water Foosball	218	Cooperation** Communication*	Self-control**		
Humongous Water Polo	204			Rapid response** Endurance** Coordination*	
Hurdles	138	Cooperation*			Running**
Jumbo Hockey	108	Cooperation**		Strength*	
Knock 'Em Down	190			Strength*	Throwing and catching**
Life Raft	216	Cooperation** Problem solving** Communication* Appropriate touch*			
Lord of the Very Big Rings	188			Keen vision** Coordination** Strength*	
Marco Ball-O	210	Cooperation** Communication*			
Mega Rugby	92			Rapid response**	Throwing and catching** Running*
Merry-Go-Round-and-Round	198	Cooperation (riders and ride masters)** Trust (riders)*		Strength (ride masters)** Endurance (ride masters)*	
Nine-Person Ball Pass	167			Coordination** Strength** Rapid response*	
Octopus	222	Cooperation*		Coordination**	
Orbit	66	Cooperation**		Coordination** Strength*	
Parachute Ball	70	Cooperation** Adaptability* Communication*	Self-control*	Keen vision** Rapid response** Strength*	
Ping Pong Ball and a Fish Bowl	178	Cooperation*	Self-control*	Keen vision** Strength**	
Planet Pass	55	Cooperation**		Strength** Rapid response*	
Poof-a-Ball	175	Cooperation**		Strength*	
Rock-and-Roll-Off	183	Cooperation**		Coordination*	

Game	Page number	Social skills	Personal behavior skills	Perceptual and physical skills	Basic motor skills
Roll-a-Row	180			Keen vision** Coordination*	
Rolling Pin	58	Appropriate touch** Trust*	Self-control**		
Rolling Relays	140	Cooperation**		Strength*	
Ships Ahoy	220	Cooperation** Communication** Trust*			
Shoot the Diameters	43	Cooperation**	Self-control*	Strength**	Throwing and catching**
Sizable Shot Put	152	Cooperation** Problem solving*		Strength**	
Smack-A-Mole	194	Cooperation*		Coordination** Keen vision*	Throwing and catching**
Small-Ball Ricochet	165			Keen vision** Rapid response*	Throwing and catching**
Super Spin	171	Cooperation*		Strength**	
Swim-Overs	206	Cooperation** Problem solving*			
Swim-Unders	208			Endurance** Strength*	
Tilt-A-World	200	Trust** Communication*			
Titanic Tennis	110	Cooperation**		Coordination** Strength*	
Towering Team Handball	98	Cooperation*		Rapid response**	Throwing and catching**
Triple Bounce	148			Coordination** Strength**	Running*
Two-Minute Hoop Bounce	169	Cooperation** Communication*		Rapid response** Coordination*	
Ultimate Ultimate	106	Cooperation**		Endurance*	Running**
Wacky Wall Ball	116				Throwing and catching** Running*
Wallies	132			Rapid response** Keen vision*	Throwing and catching**
Water Bomber	212	Cooperation*		Coordination** Rapid response**	
World-Record Dunking	214	Problem solving** Cooperation*			

Preface

Do you have any large activity balls like Pilates balls or cage balls in your equipment closet? You may know the exercise benefits of these kinds of balls, but do you know how much fun you and a group of participants can have playing with them?

Great Games for Big Activity Balls is for teachers, recreation leaders, camp counselors, and others with access to a large, inflatable activity ball who are looking for new activities. These games will engage people of all sizes, ages, and ability levels in creative, inclusive, large-scale fun.

Great Games for Big Activity Balls contains instructions, safety tips, and useful hints for an almost limitless variety of activities with a large, inflatable activity ball. These games come from our decades of experience organizing and leading play sessions with participants from all walks of life. The games and activities described in this book are unique because they are the most fun and successful when played with an activity ball that is larger than life.

Because most participants have never played with a big activity ball, this book shares tips and pointers on making the activities safe and enjoyable, so that everyone involved has fun, including you! Safety is crucial to the success of this type of play. Games that are played safely can be enjoyed over and over again.

Part I introduces the concept of a big activity ball and addresses logistical concerns. Chapter 1 provides some great reasons to play with a big activity ball. Read all the way to the end if you are looking for some fanciful themes to employ when designing your event. We are sure the ideas will inspire you to come up with even more creative motifs. Chapter 2 covers all the practical details for making the most of this fantastic piece of equipment. It also provides guidelines on buying, storing, maintaining, and repairing a big activity ball.

The seven chapters of part II describe the various games you can play with a big activity ball.

- Chapter 3 is a collection of fun, and often funny, activities that can only be played with a big activity ball.
- Chapter 4, the big sports section, continues in a more familiar vein with adaptations of popular ball games like baseball, soccer, and basketball. These really big versions of well-known sports challenge players to demonstrate their athletic skills in new ways.
- Chapter 5 helps you modify traditional playground games for the special qualities of a big activity ball.
- Chapter 6 shows you how to stage a fun and funny track-and-field event with big activity balls.
- Chapter 7 helps you and your group make your mark in the *Guinness Book of World Records,* or at least have a great time trying.
- Chapter 8 provides guidelines for hosting your own giant carnival. This fun-filled approach to big equipment engages children in safe and compelling physical challenges that are inspired by carnival games and rides.
- Chapter 9 shares ideas for playing with a large activity ball in a swimming pool or lake.

Photos of play groups in different settings tie the themes together and show you and your players just how much fun these activities can be.

In short, *Great Games for Big Activity Balls* is a complete resource of fun things to do with a really big piece of equipment.

Have any success stories you'd like to share? Did we leave out your favorite game or variation? Please feel free to contact us at bigactivityball@toddstrong.com.

Acknowledgments

We would like to thank all of the organizations and people who helped make this book possible. The following companies provided the large activity balls and other pieces of equipment seen in the photographs: Gopher Sports, Palos Sports, Omnikin, Sissel, and Sportime. See chapter 2 for contact information for these and other companies.

We would also like to thank the students and staff of Sir James Douglas Elementary School and Tecumseh Elementary, both in Vancouver, British Columbia.

PART

I

Learning About Big Activity Balls

Are you and your colleagues thinking of getting a big activity ball but are wondering if the purchase is worth the time, money, and effort? Perhaps you already have access to a big activity ball but are not sure how to use it. Maybe you are accustomed to your big activity ball, but would like some additional ideas for your players. Part I discusses the following topics:

- Having fun with a big activity ball
- Using a big activity ball as the centerpiece for an event
- Enhancing special events with big activity ball games
- Planning and leading games sessions with a big activity ball
- Staying safe while playing big games
- Buying, storing, and maintaining a big activity ball

Big Activity Ball Games

Huge Benefits, Huge Fun

No single object has inspired more people to play games than the ball. Balls are used in so many sports and recreational activities that it would be hard to list them all on one page. Imagine all of the fun activities people play with a ball, and then multiply that number by a factor of 10 or more.

Benefits of Playing Games With Big Activity Balls

Playing with a big activity ball reminds many people of a time when they were much younger and smaller. Do you remember being so small that you struggled to hold and to shoot a basketball? Childhood memories of an experience you perhaps forgot long ago will come flooding back as you play games with a big activity ball: that of feeling dwarfed by the size of the ball.

Young children love playing with a ball that is bigger than they are. A big activity ball can provide hours of fun for groups of every age, size, and ability level.

Focus on the Fun

The novelty of such a big ball adds to players' fun. Standard, familiar games are refreshed to appear like new when players try them out on a much bigger scale. They forget their preconceptions about familiar games as the scale of play is increased many times over.

Promote Cooperation

The process of figuring out how to play games with big activity balls creates an infectious cooperative spirit among players, even in games that are traditionally viewed as competitive. Players tend to help each other out, even when they are playing on opposing teams. This attitude of teamwork can continue throughout other games and activities.

Renew Creativity

Although this book provides over 70 great games and activities for play with a big activity ball, please don't feel that you must limit yourself to the games outlined here. All players who use big activity balls discover other possibilities that are particular to their needs. For example, do you have a special adaptation of the game of table tennis for a big activity ball? We'd like to hear about your fun experiences and creative efforts. You can find our e-mail address at the end of the book's preface.

Have you noticed how one little new idea or perspective can open you up to other novel concepts? The simple act of changing the scale of the ball can stimulate your creative process. Playing the games in this book will likely inspire you and your players to find innovative ways to incorporate the big activity ball into other events.

Step Away From the Traditional Role of Referee

These games help you step out of the traditional role of umpire and referee with your players. Instead of being locked into the umpire's role of making sure that your players follow well-known rules correctly, this book allows you to assume other roles like demonstrator and adjuster of games.

In the first role, you explain and demonstrate the new games to the players so that they can become participants. Present these games in as whimsical a fashion as you like. The book has lots of suggestions for playful ways to start the game. Feel free to use these ideas, or come up with your own.

The other role, which you share with the players, is that of game adjuster. An obvious way to adjust a game is to modify the boundaries to best match the sizes and abilities of the players. Tweaking the area of play to maximize the fun for all involved is an art that you and your players will develop quickly. Another way to adjust a game is to slightly alter the role of one or more players. Because many games involve a flexible number of players, modifying the roles and numbers to enhance the group's experience will soon become second nature to you.

Costs and Benefits

Big activity balls range in cost from $15 U.S. for a soft PVC ball that is approximately 3 feet (1 m) in diameter to several hundred U.S. dollars for a big cage ball that is 6 feet (approximately 2 m) in diameter. When properly cared for, these balls last for years and provide countless hours of fun for your players. The value of adding this exciting piece of equipment to your games repertoire is usually well worth the cost.

Funny Games and Meaningful Challenges

All the games in this book are funny because the idea of playing a game with an extremely big ball is funny, unusual, and unique. These games depart from traditional sports, playground games, and anything familiar. In addition, the games in this book are fun to play because they offer meaningful challenges that can be taken seriously despite the novelty of playing with such oversized equipment. The challenges are physical, social, and intellectual, and they involve the whole person.

The physical aspects of the challenges are fairly obvious. Controlling a big activity ball is never easy, even for adults. The games' social challenges come from a consistent emphasis on both collaborative and competitive teamwork. Groups must discover how to play together, blending all their various skills, abilities, and personalities into one team. Adjusting to the scale of the games and providing accommodations for unusual circumstances provide intellectual challenges. For example, how will your group navigate the logistics of playing rather ordinary games with an object that is extraordinarily large?

Scale of the Game

Increasing the scale of standard games that use much smaller balls (like handball, tennis, or soccer) by 5, 10, or even 20 times is inherently funny, and is both mathematically and conceptually interesting. To keep the game fun and functional for everyone, players must adapt their expectations, rules, and goals to the larger scale of the ball.

You can alter the scale of every game in this book, from warm-up activities to large-group games, for your specific needs.

- -

Some Additional Thoughts on Scale

Some people define *art* as that which allows the audience to experience things in a new way. Changing the scale of an everyday, frequently viewed object makes art out of standard games by turning the ordinary into the extraordinary. Claes Oldenburg makes art by exaggerating scale in his famous sculptures of objects such as a giant typewriter eraser, a massive clothes pin, and an immense lipstick tube.

In essence, this book examines what you can accomplish by changing the scale of one object, a ball. Here are some of the specific benefits of altering the scale of the ball:

○ *Novelty.* Activities that may have become stale are refreshed when you look at them in a new way. Well-known games that may bore your players in their traditional format become new and exciting with a big activity ball.

○ *Leveling the playing field.* When your players attempt a giant version of an old game, they all begin as novices. Superstars that may have gained expertise in the traditional version of the game begin this new rendering of the game at the same skill level as everybody else. This change in roles eases pressure for players who feel they must perform at a peak level all of the time and allows them to have more fun. By the same token, because everyone is adapting to the new scale of the game, players less skilled in traditional games may feel less intimidated by their teammates.

○ *Engaging the whole player.* Adapting a familiar game for play with an oversized piece of equipment requires an entire spectrum of social, intellectual, and physical skills. Imagination, creativity, sensitivity to others, agility, and problem solving all become part of the play experience.

Changing just one aspect of a game affects all the others. Consider the game of soccer (or football for folks outside of the United States and Canada). Traditionally, two teams of 11 members play on a rectangular field that ranges in size from 54 by 100 meters to 75 by 110 meters. The standard ball has a circumference between 27 and 28 inches (69 and 71 cm) and a diameter of approximately 9 inches (23 cm). The game also has rules that limit the ways that players interact with the ball. For example, one familiar rule is that the only players permitted to use their hands when the ball is in play are the goalies.

Begin by changing one aspect of this game, the size of the ball. Instead of using a standard-sized ball, try playing with a ball with a diameter of 6 feet (approximately 2 m). How does this change affect the other components of the game?

- The first change you must make is to allow the players in the field to make contact with the ball with any part of their bodies, not just their feet. It is very hard for one person to move a ball this large by kicking it with one foot, so players should be allowed to use their hands, arms, and chests as well. In fact, the best way to move such a large ball down the field is for several players to simultaneously push the ball with their bodies.

- Another obvious change is to increase the number of players on each team. Instead of 11 players per team, giant soccer or football games can have several hundred players on each side.

- Because a giant ball might not fit under all goalposts, indicate the scoring area with a long end line.

- Sometimes the ball bounces over the players' heads, either as an unexpected consequence of players from opposite teams pushing the ball at the same time, or as an intentional strategy to move the ball over the opponents' heads. That's OK. When this happens, players quickly adjust their strategy from that of banging against a giant, earth-bound ball to a collective group effort of keeping the ball aloft by slapping it with a multitude of hands. Giant overhead soccer is fun, too.

- Perhaps the most fascinating change is the shift from competition to fair play and support for the underdog. Often, as the ball approaches one of the goal lines, many players spontaneously switch teams to keep the ball in play and to prevent a goal from being scored.

All of these changes are created by manipulating just one aspect of the game, by increasing the size of the ball.

Continue this train of thought by imagining you are decreasing the scale of the game. Instead of making the ball much larger, shrink it down to the size of a table-tennis ball. How would that change affect the rules and procedures for the game?

- The number of players would be greatly reduced. A soccer or football game played with such a small ball would involve only one or two players per team.

○ Instead of using their feet to kick the ball, the players should use some sort of a paddle.

○ A game with a small ball should be played in a much smaller area than a standard soccer field.

In fact, a very successful small-scale adaptation of soccer exists. It's called foosball, and it can be found in arcades, recreation centers, and playrooms across the globe.

Changing the scale of the equipment is a great way to make classic activities fresh and new. Try playing pick-up sticks with cardboard tubes that are 12 feet (approximately 4 m) long, instead of with the standard pieces that are the size of chopsticks. Imagine using 100 meters of clothesline to play a giant version of cat's cradle. In the standard version, two players play with both hands. In other words, they use 20 fingers between them. In the giant version, 20 players simulate the four hands, with each person representing one finger.

Adapting Games for Your Group

The key to crafting effective challenges is to make them appropriate for your players. If the game is too challenging, your participants may become frustrated, anxious, or unwilling to participate. If the game is not challenging enough, the players will become bored. The boundaries and rules of these games are flexible, so you can adjust the level of difficulty to match the needs of your particular play group. This book offers many suggestions for modifying the games so they are appropriate for your group.

One reason games with extremely big activity balls are so successful is that they are funny, which makes it easier for players to take on a challenge. Humor makes difficult tasks appealing and boring activities intriguing. It also helps players become more engaged in the game.

Fun is crucial to having successful games and being an effective leader. However, people are entertained by different things at the various stages of their lives. You must tailor the challenges for the abilities and interests of your players. Like a good comedian, when sharing these games, you must find a humor that is appropriate for your audience, whether their interests are mixed or uniform. Providing fun and humor greatly increases your chances for success with your players.

Funny Ways to Teach Games and Themes

There are many ways to teach a new game. Unfortunately, most leaders employ the least-effective method: they ask the players to stand still and listen while they explain each rule. This method doesn't work, both because most players forget 95% of what is said by the time the game begins, and because they don't have fun during the explanation. If the players are bored during the explanation of the rules, they may expect to be bored during the game as well.

How many fun and different ways can a game be taught? You could teach a game without using words or using only imaginary words. You could also teach a game by inviting other people to make up the rules. For example, try saying, "We're going to play a game of Extremely Large Soccer. No one knows how to play this game because it doesn't formally exist. The only thing we know is that we have this extremely big activity ball, and we want to play soccer with it. Does anyone have any ideas?"

These are all good teaching methods that invite fun and challenge both the leaders and the players. Start with the games in this book that you think will be the easiest for you to explain and for your players to understand, and then add your own fun to the game description. Create a shared framework for interpreting a game that includes something both you and your players find funny or silly.

You can use each of the book's seven game chapters as a theme for a day, a week, or even a month of activity. The games chapters are engaging and humorous, and will help you choose themes that stimulate both intellectual and emotional participation. Your themes can involve anything from costumes and uniforms to specialized ways of talking and acting. Using humor creates an emotionally engaging and safe environment where players of every skill level can take the game less seriously. As a result, players will have more fun. Remember that themes should both focus on a particular kind of game and explain in a creative and humorous way why the ball is so large.

Introduce a new theme to your players with each new chapter, a fantasy that puts the games in the context of *half-belief.* Play theorists use this term to describe a temporary suspension between reality and fantasy that supports play. An example of half-belief is the saying, "Step on a crack, and you'll break your mother's back!" Most children do not actually believe they will damage their mothers' backs if they step on a crack in the sidewalk, but the myth sets up a fun challenge.

The Secret History of the Extremely Big Activity Ball

One aspect of a good theme is a creative and humorous explanation of the size of the equipment. When you first introduce the big activity ball to the players, invite them to make up a secret history of the ball. Here are some imaginary stories of origin to get you started:

- According to Norse mythology, the gods gave the extremely big activity ball to the elves to humble them into accepting the limits of their mortality by poking fun at their diminutive size. In defiance, the elves created games with the giant ball that demonstrated their powers and celebrated their service to the human race.

- The Egyptians invented the extremely big activity ball for the Sun Games shortly after Tutankhamen's reign ended in an effort to demonstrate man's superiority to Ra the sun god. Later, when the Greeks came to power, the Sun Games became the Olympic Games.

- Roskosmos, the Russian space agency, created the extremely big activity ball to help cosmonauts develop low-gravity skills.

- The ancient people of England produced the extremely big activity ball for the game of extremely large golf— Stonehenge was the 17th hole.

- A Rogerian child psychologist who believed that play with larger balls contributed to greater self-esteem developed the extremely big activity ball.

- Dinosaurs near the end of the Cretaceous age played with the extremely big activity ball to prepare their offspring for their roles as egg-stealing lizards.

- The military invented the extremely big activity ball for use in war zones to alter the enemy's perception of the soldiers' size and intent. The enemy thought that the soldiers out playing with the ball were smaller than they actually were.

- The Greek artist who made the statue of Atlas marketed the extremely big activity ball as a way to get rid of the extra balls he had made for the model to hold.
- Leonardo da Vinci invented the extremely big activity ball before he realized that he needed hot air in the balloons to make them soar.
- The extremely big activity ball was invented in the early days of TV when cameras weren't powerful enough to transmit balls of regular size.
- The Myopians—strong, tall people with very bad eyesight—created the extremely big activity ball.

The Fantastic History of Games for the Extremely Big Activity Ball

You can create a positive and constructive event for your entire school or community with any of the game chapters in this book. Invent a historical fantasy for your chosen chapter to provide a graphic and conceptual theme for the event. The following histories correspond to the different game chapters.

- *Extremely Big Cooperative Games (event for chapter 3).* During the early days of humankind, when the Neanderthals were still major contenders for the future of the race, the Homo sapiens hosted events with extremely big activity balls for the Neanderthals. They wished to either prove to the Neanderthals how superior they were, or to persuade them to cooperate with and join the Homo sapiens. In an earlier prehistoric version, the Neanderthals claimed to have invented large-scale cooperative games in a final, desperate attempt to stop the Homo sapiens' warlike behavior.

- *Extremely Big Sports (event for chapter 4).* Some believe extremely big sports are of extraterrestrial origin, and were first recorded by the Incas. The sport was known in the Inca language as *the alien games.* However, the Incas thought the games were played with rocks and never discovered the properties of the inflatable ball. Instead, they attributed great powers to the aliens, whom they called the *boulder-bouncers.*

- *Extremely Big Playground Games (event for chapter 5).* Invented by British children during World War II, the extremely big playground games were originally played with barrage balloons that had lost some of their buoyancy. Since the barrage balloons were so large, the games were clearly visible to airplanes flying overhead. Consequently, the games began to be played as an act of defiance, a symbolic gesture of the indomitable spirit of the British people. Sadly, before the close of the war, every barrage balloon had to be brought back into service, and the extremely big playground games were forgotten.

● *Extremely Big Athletic Games (event for chapter 6).* Modern day track-and-field events share much of their traditions and pageantry with the Olympics. According to ancient Greek myth, however, predating even the first Olympic Games were the Titanic Tournaments. The Titans were giants who ruled over ancient Greece before the time of Zeus and Hera. Of course, all of their athletic contests were equally gigantic. The pole that the Titans used for pole vaulting, for example, was made out of an entire cypress tree. Eventually, people forgot about these Titanic contests and today we have the Olympic Games and other track-and-field events at the local, regional, national, and international levels.

● *Extremely Big World Records (event for chapter 7).* Before written language was created, the ancients held large-scale public events to explain new rules to the people. In order to help people remember these new rules, the strongest and most able among them opened each session by performing an amazing act with an extremely big activity ball that shocked people into paying attention.

● *Extremely Big Carnival (event for chapter 8).* The extremely big carnival originated during the latter days of the Roman Games (the Ludi Romani). The games were held in cities without coliseums to get people excited about making the pilgrimage to the great game theaters. To make the carnivals as spectacular as the games themselves, the Romans used large objects to attract people from miles around. The extremely big carnival roamed from village to village, gathering crowds of players and spectators. The carnival decreased in popularity during the Holy Roman Empire when the large-ball games were only allowed in coliseums, then disappeared entirely during the Protestant Reformation.

● *Extremely Big Water Games (event for chapter 9).* Though much has been made of the connection between man and porpoises, only the ancient Alaskans knew the secret of befriending the great whales. By going out into the ocean and playing what they called the *whale games,* or games with huge, inflated sealskins, the ancient Alaskans lured the curious whales into participating in their spirited games of dodgeball and soccer (or football in countries outside of North America).

Using a Big Activity Ball in Your Everyday Play Time

Using a big activity ball involves more than just throwing out some playground balls for people to enjoy. The differences create many of the reasons why playing with a big activity ball is so much fun. Here are some tips to help make the experience safe and enjoyable for everybody.

Lesson Logistics

Here are a few logistical tips to keep in mind. You should sequence your lesson or program for large groups and public events. Begin with an activity in which participants bring out the balls from the place where they are stored. Continue with the theme's featured games, and then finish with an activity in which participants put the balls away again. These three steps will ensure that the players have the maximum amount of time to have fun. You should also appoint one supervisor for each big activity ball out in the field.

New Games, New Players

If the players are new to the big activity ball experience, you should introduce the game in stages and explain each stage a few rules at a time. Begin with games that all participants can play safely, understand easily, and reinvent as needed. For example, the cooperative games in chapter 3 allow the players to get a feel of the ball; how to bounce it high or back and forth, and how to push, kick, or jump on it.

The best introduction for a big activity ball activity is a demonstration:

- Players who already have become familiar with a particular game can perform for others.

● Ask players from one group to help you teach an activity to another group. They can give expert demonstrations, act as referees, or invite other people to come and play.

● Each time you play with the ball, introduce a few variations, and then invite players to make up their own.

Extremely Big Events

You can also use your big activity ball to help build a feeling of camaraderie, both within your play group and between your group and the greater community. Any of the games from this book would work well as part of an extremely large community event. Having a relay team dribble a big activity ball the entire length of the annual parade route in your community would generate some excitement, particularly if you periodically bounce the ball up to some of the parade watchers to let them take a turn. The following situations describe how using a big activity ball can enhance your communal experience.

Natural Spectacle

All of the games in this book are as much fun to watch as they are to play. Because they employ a huge ball 3, 4, or even 6 feet (approximately 1 m, 1.2 m, or 2 m) in diameter, these games are natural spectacles. Because of their size, big activity balls advertise themselves. In addition to their role in games, they can also be used for public demonstrations and celebrations of the human spirit in community events. Is there a ribbon-cutting ceremony planned to inaugurate a new building? Let the big activity ball roll across the ribbon to cut it. Or organize a team of human statues to take turns posing as Atlas holding the big activity ball up in the air to bring some additional interest to a booth you have at a community fair.

The following four chapters are devoted to games that can be used for public events:

● Chapter 4, Super Sports: Traditional Games Played in a Big Way

● Chapter 6, Big Athletic Games: Large Track-and-Field Events

- Chapter 7, Ginormous World-Record Challenges: Using Your Big Activity Ball to Earn a Place in History
- Chapter 8, Very Big Midways: Giant Carnival Games

Draw from the special images and traditions of these themes to find ideas that will help you promote your event. For example, you learn that the traditional colors for an event with a carnival or circus theme are red, blue, and yellow. You may also want to introduce a circus-themed event with a big parade. Sports-themed events can feature opening ceremonies with athletic commentators.

Remember, only two things are necessary to make a huge game into a huge event:

1. You need a group of players who know how to play the game and enjoy being watched.
2. You must advertise for the event.

New Events

If your group is already familiar with big activity ball games and events, work with them to create a public spectacle, such as an event in a stadium or cafeteria, with sportscasters and full media coverage, or an extremely big tailgate party with bands and food. If the actual media can't make it to your event, then create your own media. Some players can choose to cover the event as reporters. Begin with the events that are easy to launch and can succeed with or without large audiences. Examples include a world record attempt, a carnival game, or a sports meet designed for play with big activity balls. Next, introduce the theme in a public parade or ceremony featuring extremely big activities. Finally, present the event itself, first for a small group of trainees, then for groups of a hundred or more.

Document like crazy. Work with local clubs and organizations to make a record of your event that can be published online. The larger-than-life aspect of a big activity ball makes it a great focus for promoting and marketing special events. Journalists are likely to run a piece with a photo or video clip of players actively engaged with a big activity ball because of its great amount of visual interest.

Sporting Events

Most professional sporting events include mass media, music, cheer-leaders, and halftime marches. Sporting events are just one type of public spectacle that can become even more spectacular when they involve an inflatable ball 6 feet (approximately 2 m) in diameter. Any of the games described in chapter 4 can become spectacular public events. Use traditions from well-known sporting events to make your big event even more attractive.

- Encourage your players to attempt to set new world records. For example, which child under the age of eight can make the most hits in one round of Big Baseball?
- Introduce activities like tailgate parties and concessions as people assemble for the event.
- Recruit a band and a cheerleading squad to keep the crowd excited throughout the contest. Imagine the fun that extremely large mascots could have with a big activity ball! Cheerleaders could also use huge, two-person pom-poms or bounce big activity balls to the rhythm of the marching band's complex counterpoint. Consider posting clips from their performances on the Internet.
- Give a demonstration with your extremely big ball during halftime.
- You'll also need officials to keep score and media coverage.

Parades: Olympics and Circuses

Almost every large-scale event starts with a parade to gather crowds, drum up excitement, lead people to the venue, and increase business. The Olympics begin with a parade of the athletes before the torch is passed at the opening ceremony. A parade through town traditionally announces the arrival of the circus.

Feature the extremely big activity ball in your parade as the grand marshal, the object of the whole event. You can also highlight the players and event officials by holding extremely big games in public spaces. Consider using these activities to promote your big activity ball parade or game:

- Pass the activity ball from one place to another, as in the passing of the Olympic torch. Groups of people can run a relay with the ball, hoping to set a new record for transit time. Like the pilot cars with flags and flashing lights that notify traffic of oversize loads, this activity requires spotters.

◉ Groups can bounce and roll the big activity ball in time with music.

◉ The culmination of the parade is a grand demonstration of some world-record handling of the big activity ball.

World Record Ideas

New world records can be set anywhere, at any time, and for almost any reason. Every world-record event involves spectators, officials, and displays of greatness. They happen at carnivals, circuses, and odd public events like novelty races or monster truck rallies. For example, in San Francisco, a new world record was set at the California Academy of Science's 2007 *Run Wild* event for the most people dressed as cows to complete a 10K run in less than an hour. Some world-record attempts have become public celebrations in which one community invites another to witness or partake in record setting, such as a contest to establish a new world record in stone-skipping.

It's easy to market attempts to set a world record. Journalists are always interested in local news that is global in nature. World-record efforts make a carnival or sports event more exciting, especially if they involve an extremely big activity ball that draws public attention by virtue of its sheer size.

You can host these events anywhere and at any time as long as you have contestants, judges, and people to document the event with pictures, videos, and written articles. You can use the extremely big activity to invite people to attempt larger communal records. For example, how long can 12 people bounce a ball that is 6 feet (approximately 2 m) in diameter? How high can they bounce it?

Making Big Events Memorable

Big activity balls are not just great pieces of equipment for all sorts of games for all sorts of players. They can also be used as tools to help your events be more interesting. Although any game played with an extremely big activity ball is inherently special, here are some resources for making your event even more spectacular:

◉ If you like to be theatrical, you should introduce your event with a theme. After playing a couple of games, introduce creative variations. Work with your players to create a culminating event for the community in an outside venue.

◉ Encourage the players to design their own theme for an event, complete with fantasy, history, and culture. Imagine, for example, a Big Neanderthal Soccer tournament. Does it warm your heart a little?

◉ Decorate the ball with advertising for the event. Use painter's tape to include information on the date, sponsors, and location.

◉ Involve musicians and artists in a parade, with teams of uniformed, local heroes rolling balls through the streets.

◉ Borrow from similar public events. Take advantage of every medium and metaphor used in conjunction with the Olympics, world-record attempts, circus performances, rock concerts, and other large-scale, public affairs.

◉ Mark off a section of your performance space with chairs and benches. Stage a spectator activity demonstrating one of the games that will be played at the event to advertise for the big day.

◉ Use ideas from chapter 7 to conduct formal attempts to set world records. What's the greatest number of people who can bounce a huge activity ball in the street? How many times can a group bounce the ball in 90 seconds?

◉ Dream big. Invite star athletes from a local or professional team to compete in events with extremely big activity balls.

Summary

A big activity ball is a wonderful addition to your play equipment. Use it to keep classic games fresh and new. A special ball helps you step out of the traditional leader's role of umpire and interact with your players in new ways. Changing the size of the ball can help you think of creative and fun adaptations for all your players.

CHAPTER

2

The Nuts and Bolts of Using a Big Activity Ball

Big activity balls are so much fun that they tempt leaders as well as players. To be sure, the players will excitedly enter into the spirit of play, but you'll be surprised how difficult it is for you to watch from the sidelines with a cup of coffee. After all, who wouldn't get excited about playing with a really big ball?

Selecting and Maintaining the Activity Ball

If you already have and use a big activity ball, you know how much fun they are. Don't skip this chapter entirely, though. As well as discussing different sizes and styles of big activity balls and where to find them, we share tips on how to care for them.

What Size of Activity Ball Do I Want?

The size of your activity ball is a matter of personal preference. The games and activities in this book can accommodate balls that range in size from soft PVC balls that are 3 feet (1 m) in diameter to cage balls that are 6 feet (2 m) in diameter.

If you work with small children, choose a ball that is 40 inches (1 m) in diameter at most. A 40-inch ball will seem huge to most young children. If the participants in your play group are older and bigger, consider using a larger ball. You can have fun with balls of almost any size, but the 6-foot (2-m) balls are definitely impressive.

In addition to the size, you should consider the weight of the ball. Omnikin brand balls are noticeably lighter than other styles of a similar size. There are both advantages and disadvantages to lighter balls. For example, they are affected by gusts of wind more than their heavier counterparts. On the other hand, lighter balls are preferable for playing volleyball or bouncing in a parachute.

What Style of Activity Ball Do I Want?

Big activity balls come in a variety of styles. Would you like your ball to look like a baseball, a basketball, or a soccer ball? Other balls have a rainbow of colored panels.

Where Do I Find an Activity Ball?

This section lists companies that sell big activity balls. The companies are listed alphabetically with their addresses, phone numbers, and Web sites, which were current at the time of publication. Of course, all this information is subject to change. Please contact the suppliers directly for their most recent prices and product updates.

Companies differ in the types of warranties they offer for various brands and styles of balls. Since models and warranties change, the following information is at risk of becoming dated. The suppliers listed are all reputable and have been in business for a while. Please ask suppliers about the warranty available for your chosen activity ball.

North America

Childcraft Education Corporation
P.O. Box 3239
Lancaster, PA 17604
800-631-5652
www.childcrafteducation.com

Front Row Experience
540 Discovery Bay Blvd.
Discovery Bay, CA 94514
800-524-9091(U.S.)
www.frontrowexperience.com

Gopher Sport
220 24th Ave. NW
P.O. Box 998
Owatonna, MN 55060

800-533-0446
507-451-4755 (International)
www.gophersport.com
According to a company representative, Gopher Sport offers a lifetime warranty on all of its equipment.

Morley Athletic Supply Company

P.O. Box 557
208 Division St.
Amsterdam, NY 12010
800-811-1931 (U.S.)
www.morleyathletic.com

Omnikin

P.O. Box 45009
8083 Boulevard du Centre-Hospitalier
Charny, Quebec G6X 3R4
Canada
800-706-6645 (from North America)
418-832-0777 (International)
www.omnikin.com

Palos Sports

11711 S. Austin Ave.
Alsip, IL 60803
800-233-5484
www.palossports.com

Sportime

3155 Northwoods Pkway.
Norcross, GA 30071
800-283-5700
770-449-5700 (International)
www.sportime.com

Lakeshore Learning Materials

2695 E. Dominguez St.
Carson, CA 90895
800-778-4456
www.lakeshorelearning.com

Sissel

P.O. Box 729
Sumas, WA 98295
888-474-7735
800-811-1355 (Canada)
www.sissel-online.com

Toledo Physical Education Supply

5101 Advantage Dr.
Toledo, OH 43612
800-225-7749
419-726-8122 (International)
www.tpesonline.com

Europe

Davies Sports

Hyde
Cheshire
SK14 4LL
+44 0845 120 4515
www.daviessports.co.uk

Australia and New Zealand

Sportime Australia

21-23 Viking Court
Cheltenham VIC 3192
1800-335-041 (in Australia)
+61 3 9555 7555 (International)
www.sportime.com.au

Yardgames

Unit 5a / 84a Old Pittwater Road
Brookvale NSW 2100
Australia
1300 76 75 21 (in Australia)
+61 (0) 2 9938 1713 (International)
www.yardgames.com.au/

The Big Game Company
P.O. Box 109 608
Newmarket, Auckland
New Zealand
0800 843 244 (in New Zealand)
www.thebiggamecompany.co.nz

How Do I Inflate an Activity Ball?

Back in the old days, we used to go to gas stations to inflate the big activity balls. The air compressors that top off automobile and bicycle tires can also inflate insanely huge activity balls. Although service station air pumps are good at delivering high-pressure air, they can only emit it in small streams. It usually took about 20 to 30 minutes to inflate a ball 6 feet (2 m) in diameter.

When the ball was finally inflated, we had to get it from the gas station to the park. We quickly learned to bring a convertible or a pick-up truck. Once they are inflated, the balls will not fit in an ordinary car. If the park was close enough to the gas station, we would roll the ball back. We usually attracted lots of attention and created a spontaneous parade along the way. Whether the inflated ball arrived in a vehicle or in a parade, the arrival tended to create a surge of enthusiasm among the players. Although it was a lot of fun, we don't recommend that method of inflating a big activity ball anymore.

Many types of smaller pumps now exist. However, most people are intimidated by the thought of using a hand or foot pump to fill such a large ball. The best and recommended method is to use a small, electric pump that is specifically designed for the task. Most companies that sell big activity balls also sell these pumps.

Practice inflating your big activity ball before the play session begins to become familiar with the most efficient technique. It is much more difficult to inflate the ball when you are surrounded by excited players who want to get their hands, feet, shoulders, and legs on the ball. Some electric pumps are quite loud, so you should wear earplugs when inflating the ball. If you're excited by the prospect of seeing your new ball, you may overlook the fact that you're holding a power tool, however small, next to your ear.

Some styles require two people to inflate the ball and seal its valve. For example, after inflation, you must quickly tie a length of cord around the valve of an Omnikin ball to seal it. You'll appreciate a second person for this stage of the inflation process. Think how much easier it is to wrap a present when someone else holds the knot on the string while you tie the bow.

Even if you can easily open and close the ball's valve by yourself, you may want someone to help you reposition the ball as it inflates. As the inside bladder gets bigger, the valve should line up with the opening in the outer cover (see figure 2.1). Before the ball is fully inflated, the cumbersome outer cover tends to flop around the ball and can be difficult for one person to control.

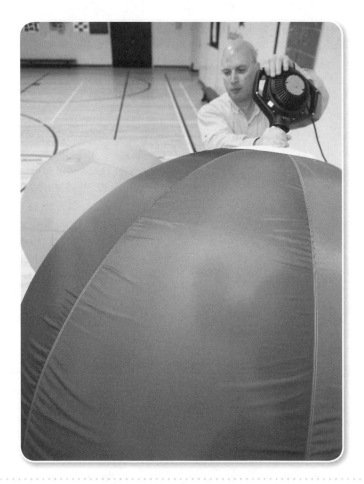

Figure 2.1 During inflation, make sure the valve on the bladder lines up with the opening of the outer skin.

Can I Overinflate the Ball?

Some people get nervous when they learn that a big activity ball needs only 2 psi, or pounds per square inch (approximately 14,000 Pa), of air pressure. Please don't be concerned about popping your equipment during the inflation process. Activity balls are very durable. Electric pumps that are designed for big activity balls will not overinflate them. Let the electric pump fill the ball until it is nice and tight. Balls with a nylon covering will become taut when they are properly inflated.

However, an electric air pump can pop a bladder. I was using an electric air pump to inflate one of the light bladders and I purposefully kept the pump going after the outer skin was taut. The bladder popped. Admittedly, the bladder was over a year old, and the warranty had expired. I'm sure I would have gotten much more use out of that particular bladder had I not tried to overinflate it.

How Do I Store a Big Activity Ball?

If you have the space, keep your ball inflated for storage. You can store it safely in an overhead cargo net that is out of reach. When you want to play, the ball is ready for you.

If you don't have the space to store an inflated ball, keep it in a duffel or sports bag with a zipper that runs along the full length of the top for easy access. If your ball has inner and outer parts, leave the bladder inside the outer covering for extra protection (see figure 2.2). Store the bag in a cool, dry location. Choose a bag that is large enough to store the pump as well so you will have all your equipment handy when you are ready to inflate the ball again.

How Do I Prevent Leaks?

If you want to keep your ball from ripping, tearing, and leaking, make sure your playing area is free of sharp objects. If you have room, your group can play indoors. Some manufacturers recommend exclusive indoor play for their brand of big activity balls. However, most balls are sturdy enough for outdoor play. Please check with your supplier to see if the ball you'd like to purchase is appropriate for your needs. If you do play outdoors, choose a clean, grassy area rather than a dirt surface. Balls can easily be punctured by pieces of broken glass and sharp sticks.

Figure 2.2 A sports bag with a large opening makes a great system to store your big activity ball and pump together.

Periodically inspect the skin of the ball to see if the stitching is holding up. The old adage, "a stitch in time saves nine," applies here. It's much easier to perform routine maintenance than to repair major damage, and it is possible to repair or replace damaged portions of a ball. Many balls come with an extra piece of nylon to sew onto the outer skin if it gets ripped. If the bladder of your ball gets punctured, you should replace it. With the proper care, big activity balls can last for years.

How Do I Repair the Outside Skin of a Big Activity Ball?

Please understand that these generic instructions have worked well for us. If your particular brand of big activity ball has specific repair instructions, please follow those instructions. The following tips apply if you have a big activity ball with an outer, nylon skin. Our preference is to use iron-on nylon patches. Turn the skin inside out and apply the patch to the inside of the skin. This way you don't have to worry about matching the color that closely.

Set an iron on medium to medium-high heat, with no steam. Place some cotton fabric between the iron and the iron-on patch and the skin of the ball. Apply heat with the iron to melt or glue the patch to the skin. If your iron-on patch matches the skin of the ball, you can turn the skin outside out and apply a second patch to the outside of the skin.

After ironing, you can also sew the patch if you like. Our patches seem to hold up well enough without sewing.

How Do I Clean a Big Activity Ball?

In the past, we cleaned big, inflated cage balls with heavy canvas skins at a self-service car wash, then left them out in the sun to dry. It is possible to separate the bladder and outer skin of the new, lighter cage balls, so you can now clean them yourself at home.

Wash the bladder outside with a garden hose. Remember that this piece is vulnerable when outside of its protective skin, so make sure you clean it in an area that is free of bits of glass or sharp burrs.

The outer skin of the activity ball can be cleaned in either a personal or commercial washing machine. You may need to take big activity balls to a Laundromat. Wash the ball on a gentle cycle with cold water, unless the accompanying instructions call for warm water. After washing, hang the covering up to air dry.

Planning for Fun

Play sessions with a big activity ball require planning and supervision. Consider the following topics: when you will inflate the ball, where you plan to play, the length of the session, the amount of players, which games to play, and how to put the ball away.

Inflating the Ball

You can save time by inflating your ball before you come to the play session. This means you can inflate the ball on your own terms, without a bunch of eager players offering to help. However, first consider the following questions: Do you have a place to store the ball until the play session? How will you transport the ball? Will a full-sized ball fit through doors? Will someone be able to supervise the ball at all times? For full information, see the previous section in this chapter, "How Do I Inflate an Activity Ball?"

Determining the Play Area

Here are some tips for choosing the location of your play session. The play area should be large enough, both horizontally and vertically, for the planned activities. For example, you must choose a room with a high ceiling for a game like Orbit. Is there anything on the ground that could injure the players or damage the ball? Scan the area for tree branches when playing outdoors.

Choosing the Games

You should make a written list of the games you've planned for the session, and keep it handy. It is a good idea to plan a couple of additional games in case you have extra time at the end of the session. Choose games that are appropriate for the number of players in your group, but remember that you can easily modify most games to accommodate groups of various sizes.

Putting the Ball Away

This book also shows you how to play with a ball as you deflate it to put it away. Chapter 3 features these games, which include Ball Surfing, Bumper Ball, and Hair Dryer. Choose one of these games for the end of the playing time if you'd like the players to help you deflate the ball. Enthusiastic players, especially young ones, always want to participate in the deflation process. If you prefer to deflate and store the ball on your own, simply wait until the players leave.

Playing Safely

One reason that people love games is that they can play them over and over. Games can only be repeated if they are played safely. If people get hurt, they won't be able to or may not want to play again. This section offers some general thoughts on safety for your big activity ball. You'll find specific considerations for each game in the safety tips section of each description.

Most importantly, the games in this book are designed to be played under supervision. We suggest that you do more as a leader than roll out a ball and observe as the players engage in free play.

Plan to play an integral, active part in the games and to stay near the big activity ball most of the time.

Most kids have a hard time controlling themselves around these big, light, round, and bouncy balls. They have an immediate urge to kick them, throw them, jump on them, lie on top of them, sit on them, or bounce on them. Children see a big activity ball as very soft, safe, and fun, and it is. However, the rest of the world isn't as soft or as safe. Gym floors and playground surfaces can be remarkably hard and unyielding. As a games leader, you should continually scan your environment to make sure the area is safe. Check outside fields for debris and inside surfaces for slipperiness. Also, watch the proximity of the players and the ball to walls, benches, bushes, or trees. Make sure your players don't run into a safety hazard.

Before you introduce a game with a big activity ball, especially if your group has never played with one, make sure everyone has had a chance to touch it. The ball's sheer size makes it almost overwhelmingly attractive to your players, who usually exhibit a desperate need to touch and discover it.

The best way to give the group an opportunity to touch the big activity ball is to play one of the cooperative, carnival, or world-record games. Most of these games focus more on controlling the ball than on winning. Players are less likely to get distracted by the heat of competition, and more likely to focus on the risks and properties of the big activity ball. This approach is especially advisable with larger activity balls. When you sense that the players are able to keep both themselves and the ball in check, they are ready to play a more physically demanding game.

As you reach the end of a session with a big activity ball, you'll probably want to put the ball away before you bring the session to a close. If you leave the ball inflated, a few players will likely begin to play with it unsupervised as they leave the area. Chapter 3 highlights some games you can play while deflating the ball.

No Ball Is an Island: Never Leave a Ball Unattended

You should never leave a big activity ball unattended while it is inflated. If you do, you will likely see the following results:

1. A seemingly slight wind will cause the ball to roll away like a sail to a place far away from you.

2. Outsiders will begin playing without your consent.

While we like to encourage spontaneous play, we have found that it is best not to allow strangers to play with big activity balls without supervision. Unsupervised players get so excited by the possibilities of the ball that they tend to disregard safety considerations.

The best way to ensure safety is to deflate the ball when you are finished with it. A large, limp bladder stuffed into a lumpy bag just isn't as tempting as a big activity ball. Even the gustiest of winds will not blow away a deflated ball. If you pack the ball up right away, you no longer need to worry about it.

If you want to take a break and use the inflated ball later, wrap it up in a parachute and tie the whole apparatus to a tree, bench, or other stationary object (see figure 2.3).

Figure 2.3 The parachute that holds this ball is tied to the goal past so a gust of wind won't cause the ball to roll away.

Remember that you must keep an eye on the ball and parachute during the break. Our years of experience in public parks have taught us that the sight of a huge ball wrapped up in a parachute piques people's curiosity. If you don't watch out, some enterprising players will figure out a way to liberate the ball from its confining parachute.

In conclusion, you should never leave big attractive activity balls like these unattended. If the ball is out where people can see it, you need to stay with it. If you have more than one big activity ball, then you'll need at least one responsible adult to supervise each ball. This doesn't mean that the leaders won't be able to have fun. It just means that the focus of your fun will be keeping your players engaged and safe.

When you're a leader, you will have more fun when your players become deeply involved and take responsibility for maintaining a fun and safe game flow. You'll experience the vicarious enjoyment of giving a child a new toy that begins with the initial delight in getting something new, then deepens into a more sustainable form of play as the child discovers all the wonderful things the toy can do.

Wow, That's an Extremely Big Activity Ball!

Another reason you should supervise big activity balls at all times is their size. These balls can be even bigger than your tallest players. Most of the time, it's fine for players to be obscured by the ball. However, if a big, enthusiastic player decides to run into the ball, it may crash into a smaller, unaware, innocent player on the other side. Because all players are focused on the ball during games, this type of accident only happens during unstructured time with the ball.

Focus on the Ball

A few of the games are designed for overhead play with the ball. Be aware that in these situations, players will look up at the ball rather than at each other. A group that is both running and sky gazing has great potential for collisions. This book aims to minimize running when the ball is handled overhead. The game of Orbit, described in chapter 3, is a good example of this. Players remain stationary while the ball is over their heads and feet when playing Orbit.

Sometimes we like to play a very loose version of Giant Soccer. When players from opposite teams bang on the ball, it frequently bounces over their heads. Soon, Giant Soccer has become Giant Mobile Volleyball. If your players can exercise discipline with the ball overhead, this situation is safe. If you feel uneasy about the situation, slow things down by switching over to the safer game of Crab Soccer, described in chapter 4.

Summary

Although you can have a lot of fun playing with a big activity ball, you must plan each session intentionally. You can't hand out big activity balls the way you might hand out playground balls at recess, because most players won't know how play safely. It is your responsibility as the leader to plan activities to be both fun and safe.

PART

II

Learning the Games

This part of the book is where the fun begins. Chapters 3 through 9 cover more than 70 games for big activity balls. The chapters highlight variations on the following themes: cooperative games, sports, playground games, track-and-field events, world records, carnivals, and water games.

The chapters are formatted to help you quickly and easily decide if a particular game is appropriate for your group and setting. They use specific categories to outline everything you need to know to lead the game. If pertinent, the following categories will appear in the description of each game:

- *Objective.* This section explains the essence of the game. For competitive games, an explanation of how to score points and win the game is provided. For noncompetitive (cooperative) games, this section sets up the group's collective goal.

- *Additional equipment.* This category highlights other pieces of equipment necessary for a game. The big activity ball is a given piece of equipment for every game in the book.

- *Safety tips.* This section notes areas of awareness for safe play.

- *Lead-ins.* This section lists activities that serve as a good introduction for a certain game. These lead-ins are simply suggestions. Use your experience to determine which activities will best prepare your group for a particular game.

● *Developmental skills.* Games that include this section help develop your group's social, behavioral, perceptual, and basic motor skills. The skills within each section are differentiated as primary or secondary. Please see the game finder for an explanation of each skill.

● *Duration of game.* If the players are having fun and if they have enough time, there really is no limit to how long these games can last. However, this section provides ideas on how long it may take your group to achieve the game's objectives. Some of the games feature rounds of play. For these games, allow enough time for each player to participate in at least one round.

● *When to play.* Some games are best played at the beginning of a play session. Others work better at the end of a play session. This section provides tips based on our experience with particular games. This category is also very open and flexible. Use your knowledge of the group to decide when a particular game would work best.

● *Follow-ups.* The activities in this section have been chosen to follow a certain game to ease transitions or help the flow of a session. Again, these games are merely suggestions. Be creative when planning follow-up activities.

● *Variations.* This section explains how to modify a given game. Variations help keep the game fresh and exciting for your players, so they should probably be spaced out over time. Groups shouldn't play a game and all its variations in the same session. Introduce a variation of a popular game at a future session to keep your players interested.

● *Teaching tips.* This is our way of passing along the experience we've gained by leading these games. These techniques and strategies will make games more fun for you and your players.

Ready for some fun? The following chapters are full of games, challenges, and activities that you and your players will love. Get out the air pump, turn the page, and start exploring the world of sports and games played on a massive scale.

3

Big Cooperative Games

Activities Designed for Big Play

The 16 games in this chapter take advantage of the larger-than-life properties of a big activity ball. They come from the New Games movement of noncompetitive play, feature cooperation, and will help you and your players discover your big activity ball's full potential.

Hip Check

Limber dancers, with hips that naturally sway and swivel to a solid beat, will love the game of Hip Check. It is also a great game for aspiring ice-hockey players who need to practice bumping members of the other team out of position.

Players stand in a loose circle, facing the center. Their goal is to use their hips to bump the ball around the circle or across its center. In the strict version of Hip Check, players must keep one foot planted on the edge of the circle. They may pivot on this planted foot up to 90 degrees to the side to meet the ball straight on. Players can show their appreciation by cheering and clapping for a particularly forceful hip check or a graceful style.

Objective

Using only their hips, players try to bounce the ball to different parts of the circle.

Additional Equipment

None

Safety Tips

None

Lead-Ins

Players should master the game Shoot the Diameters before playing.

Developmental Skills

- Primary skills include cooperation and strength.
- Secondary skills include self-control.

Duration of Game

Play this game for three to five minutes.

When to Play

Play this game near the beginning of the session.

Follow-Ups

Follow this game with a round of Donut Rolls.

Variations

In the relaxed team version of Hip Check, players may take one or two steps to meet the ball. They may also form spontaneous, temporary teams and check the ball with a partner. After checking the ball, players should return to the edge of the circle.

Teaching Tips

It's always fun to watch people succeed in this game. Well-timed hip checks that blast the ball across the circle are satisfying for both the checker and the other players. Similarly, everyone enjoys the rare moments of grace when a player demonstrates a particularly stylish hip check. Good hits that result from partnerships are even more appreciated. Well-coordinated hip checks involving two or three players are rare demonstrations of beauty and teamwork.

In a more humorous vein, the startled reaction to a hip check that doesn't quite hit the mark can be a wonderful moment for the group to share. There is a certain comedic surprise when a player uses a large amount of pelvic energy, but manages only a glancing blow or misses the ball entirely. Imperfect performances can generate a feeling of empathy and camaraderie in the group.

Donut Rolls

In the game Donut Rolls, players stand in the shape of a donut by forming two concentric circles. The players in the inner circle face out and the players in the outer circle face in. The outer circle should contain a greater number of players than the inner circle. The distance between the two circles should be slightly wider than the diameter of the big activity ball, and the space that is created will form a kind of track for the ball to roll in. Players work together to roll the ball around the space between the two circles of people.

Once the players get used to pushing the ball around the track together, they can try to set speed records. Designate a starting line at one cross section of the donut and see how fast the group can complete one lap around the track. When the players have established a benchmark, challenge them to see if they can beat that time.

Objective

Players cooperatively roll the big activity ball around the track between two concentric circles of people.

Additional Equipment

Stopwatch

Safety Tips

Make sure that players stay in their circles and stay out of the ball's path.

Lead-Ins

- Shoot the Diameters
- Hip Check

Developmental Skills

- Primary skills include rapid response and coordination.
- Secondary skills include cooperation and keen vision.

Duration of Game

Play this game for a few minutes.

When to Play

Play this game toward the beginning of the session.

Follow-Ups

Boulder Roll

Variations

When players become comfortable with the weight and momentum of the ball, they may roll the ball in the other direction. At first, you may want to cue the players verbally to change directions. After practicing for a while, players may voluntarily choose to switch directions.

Teaching Tips

This game is an excellent way to introduce the players to the size, weight, speed, and momentum of the ball. Since the players are relatively stationary for this game, most of their energy is directed toward the ball, not toward others.

Boulder Roll

This variation of Donut Rolls is reminiscent of the opening sequence in the first Indiana Jones film, when the hero runs from a giant boulder rolling down the chute of a narrow cave.

Begin the game by rolling the big activity ball inside the donut of players. Select one player from either circle by tapping a shoulder or by calling out a name. The designated player leaves the circle, enters the track between the circles of players, and runs away from the rolling ball. The group tries to roll the large ball fast enough to catch and tag the runner. If the ball tags the runner, that player chooses a successor. Runners win the game if they can complete three laps around the track without being tagged by the ball. After three laps, the victorious runner gives another player a chance to try.

Players in the circles may mix things up by changing the direction of the ball at will. Also, the runner may designate a replacement at any time by tagging another player and rejoining the circle. The newly tagged player must take off quickly to avoid being hit by the giant ball.

Objective

The group stands in two concentric circles, then tries to roll the big activity ball around the donut track fast enough to tag the designated runner. The runner flees from the ball, and tries to complete three laps before being tagged.

Additional Equipment

None

Safety Tips

The moment when a player standing in the donut formation transitions from a stationary role to an active running role is one of the more exciting and perilous parts of the game. Players must pay attention to the position of the ball when switching to the role of runner so they don't get knocked over.

Lead-Ins

Donut Rolls

Developmental Skills

◉ Primary skills include running, cooperation, and coordination.
◉ Secondary skills include keen vision.

Duration of Game

Play this game for 5 to 10 minutes.

When to Play

Play this game after the players have warmed up a bit. This can also be a good final game, since players exert lots of energy rolling and pushing the ball around.

Follow-Ups

Because this game can be very active, follow it up with less-strenuous games, such as Rolling Pin or Planet Pass.

Variations

Instead of the players chasing the runner around the circle with the ball, the runner may chase the ball as the other players push it around the circle. The runner now becomes the chaser, and has two laps to try to tag the ball.

Teaching Tips

Players should watch out for the moment when the chaser tags a new player to run. These transitional moments of change may bring about misfortune or opportunity. Of course, whether it is a misfortune or opportunity is a matter of perspective.

Shoot the Diameters

Geometry defines a *diameter* as a line that traverses a circle, passing through the center. This game, called Shoot the Diameters, allows your players to create a huge geometry lesson right on the playing field.

Players stand on the perimeter of a large circle, facing in. The ball is inside the circle. Divide the circle into four sections, as if you were slicing a pizza into four quarters. Combine the sections of players facing one another to make two teams. For the first round, the players on team A are the rollers and the players on team B are the shooters (see figure 3.1).

Two rollers standing next to each other attempt to move the large ball all the way across the circle with a single push. Their goal is for the ball to reach another set of teammates in the opposite quarter-section of the circle.

As the large ball rolls across the circle, a shooter from team B throws a sponge ball at it and tries to hit it. If the large ball rolls all the way across the circle without being hit, the rollers score a point. The rollers who received the large ball begin the next round by pushing it back across the circle to a different set of teammates.

If the sponge ball hits the large ball, or if the large ball does not make it all the way across the circle, then the teams switch roles.

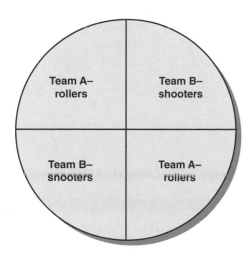

Figure 3.1 Team members line up in opposite quadrants.

Players from team B become the new rollers for this round, and take a turn pushing the large ball across the diameter. The first team to score 11 points wins.

Objective

Rollers try to push the big activity ball to teammates on the other side of the circle. Shooters try to hit the big activity ball with a foam ball.

Additional Equipment

Shooters may use one or more foam balls.

Safety Tips

Players must stay in their positions around the circle. Anyone who runs across the circle may get bowled over by the big activity ball.

Lead-Ins

This game is excellent for players who are beginners with a large ball, since it helps them master the ball's heft and momentum.

Developmental Skills

- Primary skills include cooperation, strength, and throwing and catching.
- Secondary skills include self-control.

Duration of Game

Play this game for 5 to 10 minutes.

When to Play

Play this game at the beginning of the session.

Follow-Ups

- Hip Check
- Donut Roll
- Planet Pass

Variations

Large groups may create circles that are so large that two players cannot comfortably roll the ball across with a single push. In this case, the original rollers may choose a few players to enter the circle and push the big activity ball an additional time. The rollers in the

center should be careful; if one of them gets hit by the foam ball, then the round ends, and the teams switch roles.

Teaching Tips

Players should stand still in the circle to prevent confusion when teams switch roles.

Group Dribbling

Two players stand on opposite sides of the ball and hold the palms of their hands on the upper half of the ball. The players should begin by lightly tapping the ball. With a bit of coordination, they should be able to find a common rhythm and begin bouncing the ball a couple of inches (5 cm) off the floor. Once they have established a dribble, they should try to run down the court with the ball. Players can also partner up for a relay. Half of the teams go to a preset position on the court, and pairs take turns dribbling the ball across the distance and passing it off to the next team in line.

Objective

Pairs of players coordinate their efforts to dribble the ball across a set distance.

Additional Equipment

None

Safety Tips

Although this scenario is unlikely, players must dribble the ball low to the ground so it doesn't bounce out of control and land on other players.

Lead-Ins

- Group Stretches
- Rolling Pin

Developmental Skills

- Primary skills include cooperation and coordination.
- Secondary skills include keen vision, problem solving, running, and walking.

Duration of Game

Make sure you time the activity so that all players have an opportunity to dribble the ball at least once.

When to Play

Play this game near the beginning of the session.

Follow-Ups

- Orbit
- Planet Pass
- Any game that involves the entire group

Variations

Three players attempt to dribble the ball together. They may either spread themselves evenly around the ball or take positions at three of the four quarter-sections of the ball. If they choose the latter method, they should dribble the ball toward the portion of the ball where no one is standing.

Teaching Tips

Use a ball that is proportional to the average height of your players. Players must be able to reach the top half of the ball with their hands.

Some players aren't able to coordinate their rhythm with partners as quickly as others. Remind them to listen to the sound of their hands tapping on the ball. This may help them work more closely with their partners. You can also ask their teammates to say the word *tap* each time they touch the ball to help them synchronize their dribbling. Partner up with any players who are still having trouble, and ask them to follow your movements.

Ball Crawl

Imagine you are climbing on top of the world and looking down at all of the people below. As they play Ball Crawl, the players in your group can pretend to be arctic explorers on a trek to the North Pole.

One player begins by running and jumping on top of the ball. The player must use hands and knees to maintain a steady position and to control the ball. Once on top, balanced, and comfortable, the player begins crawling. Crawling forward has the surprising effect of making the ball roll backwards. Crawling backward makes the ball roll forward. It's safer and more fun to crawl forward and make the ball roll backward.

It is quite common for players to be unable to get on top of the ball by themselves. Fortunately, this problem is easily remedied with teamwork. The player having difficulty should hug the ball, stretching both arms out above the shoulders. Two spotters stand on either side, hold that player's arms and legs against the ball, and roll the ball forward until it is underneath the player. The spotters should stop moving when the player's center of gravity is on top of the ball. The player then gets up on hands and knees.

Objective

Players take turns attempting to crawl on top of the ball.

Additional Equipment

None

Safety Tips

Players must maintain four points of contact (both hands and both knees) with the ball while on top. This is a fairly stable position. Players may not stand or kneel in an upright position without the hands touching the ball.

Spotters are more important in Ball Crawl than in any other game in this book. The spotters' goal is to prevent the ball crawler's head and neck from crashing to the ground. Spotters standing near the crawler's head must be more vigilant than those near the crawler's feet. The primary spotter should stand facing the player on top of the ball. If the player begins to slide face-first down the front of the ball, the spotter should support the player's head, neck, and shoulders. If the fall is in the other direction, away from the spotter, the player will safely land feet-first. If you are fortunate enough to have three spotters, place one on each side and in front of the ball crawler. It is rare for a player to fall off the side of the ball, but it is good to have spotters on hand just in case. It is less important to have a spotter in the rear position. If you do place a spotter behind the ball, caution that person to move out of the way if the crawler falls backward.

Lead-Ins

- Boulder Roll
- Planet Pass
- Games that involve the entire group

Developmental Skills

- Primary skills include trust and coordination.
- Secondary skills include rapid response.

Duration of Game

Time the activity so that each player can spend at least 30 seconds on top of the ball.

When to Play

Introduce the large ball to players with some warm-up games, then play Ball Crawl in the middle of the session.

Follow-Ups

- Rolling Pin
- Any game that involves the entire group

Variations

Ball Spin is a variation of Ball Crawl with a different kind of mobility. The game begins the same way, with one player positioned on top of the ball on hands and knees. Instead of crawling, the player on top remains motionless while several players holding the ball slowly spin it on its axis.

Teaching Tips

Ball Crawl is tremendously fun to play, but it has one disadvantage: only one player can be on the ball at a time. You may want to play this game when you have only a few players in a group, so people don't have to wait too long for their turns on top of the ball.

Group Stretches

In this exercise, use the ball as a giant, gentle stretching rack for the group. Your group's goal is for all participants to maintain their balance around the ball while getting a nice upper-body stretch.

Two or three participants stand around the ball and clasp wrists with one another over the top. With a slow, coordinated effort, the players simultaneously lift their feet off the ground and hang from the side of the ball. This exercise provides a chance to rest and relax after more active games.

Objective

Players should work together to maintain balance while hanging from the ball.

Additional Equipment

None

Safety Tips

Since this game doesn't involve running with the ball, it is very safe. All participants should have a steady grip on their partners' wrists before lifting their feet. Even if players lose their grip, they will simply slide off the ball and land safely on their feet.

Lead-Ins

- Boulder Roll
- Eclipse

Developmental Skills

- Primary skills include trust and strength.
- Secondary skills include self-control.

Duration of Game

Rounds lasting 10 to 30 seconds should give participants a good stretch.

When to Play

Use this exercise in the middle of the play session.

Follow-Ups

- Orbit
- A more active game

Variations

Depending on the relative size of the players and the ball, you might try a Group Stretch with four players. If the proportions between the diameter of the ball and the height of your players match, the four players can form a small circle of joined arms and hands, a sort of Arctic Circle, around the top portion of the ball. In this variation, players don't have to reach all the way across the top of the ball to grab their neighbors' wrists. The four-player variation requires more coordination to maintain steady balance, but that's the fun part.

If your players have mastered balance in the simple group stretch, they may try a gentle version of Merry-Go-Round-and-Round. Players alternate between pushing off and hanging from the side of the ball, and resting with their feet on the ground.

Teaching Tips

This exercise works best when players of similar size are grouped together to stretch on the ball.

Planet Pass

Players form two lines, with the lines facing each other. All players except two (one on each end) slowly lie down on their backs. Their heads should form one line down the middle and their feet should form two parallel lines on either side.

The players lying on the ground hold their hands straight up, above their faces, and pass the ball back and forth along the line. The players standing at each end of the line act as human bumpers. It may help to have a spotter on each side of the line to guide the ball back if it rolls toward the passers' feet.

Objective

Players work cooperatively to pass the ball back and forth on the line while lying down.

Additional Equipment

None

Safety Tips

Players should have their hands and arms in the proper position before the ball is placed on the line.

Lead-Ins

- Rolling Pin
- Group Dribbling

Developmental Skills

- Primary skills include cooperation and strength.
- Secondary skills include rapid response.

Duration of Game

The game should last a couple of minutes.

When to Play

Play this game toward the beginning of the session.

Follow-Ups

Since the players will get some rest while lying on their backs, follow this exercise with a more active game such as Orbit or Giant Soccer. Rolling Pin is another good follow-up because most of the players are already in a line.

Variations

In the game Infinite Planet Pass, players stand up as soon as they have passed the ball, run to the other end of the line, and then lie down again. The path for the passing ball can continue as long as you have open space.

Teaching Tips

Planet Pass is a great game for players of all energy levels and abilities. The players get to rest as they lie on their backs. They also get a slight upper-body workout as they collectively pass the ball with their arms and hands.

Rolling Pin

Before they put all sorts of wonderful treats into the oven, bakers frequently use a rolling pin to flatten the dough. This game is for any player who has ever wondered what it feels like to be the dough.

The majority of players lie down on their bellies, shoulder to shoulder, forming a long line of bodies that symbolizes the dough. Two players in the role of bakers stand at one end of the line with a giant cage ball, which symbolizes a rolling pin, between them. One baker stands near peoples' heads and the other baker stands near their feet. The bakers carefully roll the ball down the line of players, as if using a rolling pin to stretch out the dough. If they feel the dough isn't thin enough after the first pass, they may choose to roll the pin over the line a second time.

Objective

Two players roll the ball over a line of willing participants who are lying down on their stomachs.

Additional Equipment

None

Safety Tips

None

Lead-Ins

- Hip Check
- Boulder Roll

Developmental Skills

- Primary skills include appropriate touch and self-control.
- Secondary skills include trust.

Duration of Game

Play this game for a couple of minutes.

When to Play

Play this game during the middle of the session.

Follow-Ups

Continue play with an active game like Orbit.

Variations

In the variation called Infinite Rolling Pin, the bakers never run out of dough. After the ball rolls over the people at the head of the line, they get up, run to the other end of the line, and lie down again. If the individuals who make up the dough move quickly and the bakers roll the giant pin slowly, the line may stretch out forever.

Teaching Tips

Players tend to enjoy being in the role of the dough more when they are vocal. They may call out the type of baked treat they imagine they are being rolled into. Some players may choose to verbalize how they feel as the giant ball rolls over them.

Airmail

· · · · · · · ·

Players divide into two teams; one team controls the big activity ball and the other team gets a small foam ball. The team with the big activity ball stands in the center of the play area and the other team forms a circle around them. Players in the center take turns throwing the big activity ball to their teammates. Each time the inner team throws the big activity ball up in the air, a member of the outer team tries to throw the foam ball to a teammate on the other side of the circle. The airmail delivery package (the foam ball) must travel over the big activity ball without hitting it.

The outer team scores points by making an airmail delivery, or successfully passing the package from one side of the circle to the other. The inner team scores points if the package hits the activity

ball or if the players on the other side fail to catch the package. The inner team's strategy is to throw the big activity ball so high that it blocks the package's path. The big activity ball may also block a player's view who is trying to catch the package.

Objective

The outer team attempts to pass a foam ball over the big activity ball to teammates standing on the other side of the circle. The inner team tries to block the foam ball's path by throwing the big activity ball up in the air.

Additional Equipment

Foam ball

Safety Tips

None

Lead-Ins

Boulder Roll

Developmental Skills

- Primary skills include throwing and catching and strength.
- Secondary skills include keen vision.

Duration of Game

Play this game for 5 to 10 minutes.

When to Play

Play this game in the middle of the session.

Follow-Ups

- Eclipse
- Planet Pass

Variations

Sometimes a sneaky mail delivery person tries to pass the package underneath the big activity ball. The foam ball's postal route may even include a bounce on the ground. Postal workers are allowed to bounce the foam ball once in this variation. They should be rewarded with applause for carrying out this risky move successfully.

Teaching Tips

The game of Airmail requires players to cooperate quite a bit. The players on the inner team must work together to loft the ball as high as they can. The players on the outer, or postal-delivery, team must communicate with each other to ensure a successful delivery.

Eclipse

Eclipse is a game that simulates the rare occurrence when one heavenly body blocks another. This version of dodgeball is played with two teams: the galactic forces and the moons. The majority of players join the galactic forces team, while only two or three players are on the moon team at a time.

The galactic-force players stand in a large circle, facing in. The two or three moon players take the big activity ball that symbolizes the sun into the center of the circle and place it on the ground. While the human moons don't have to orbit the sun in a regular fashion, the gravitational field of the large ball does keep them from drifting too far away.

The galactic-force players stand on the perimeter of the circle, which symbolizes the far reaches of the solar system. From there, they launch foam-ball asteroids across the solar system at the players in the center, trying to create cosmic collisions between the asteroids and the human moons. The moons avoid being hit with the asteroids by hiding behind the sun, or creating eclipses that shield themselves from the asteroids.

Galactic-force players don't always have to aim an asteroid directly at a moon. Members of the galactic forces may toss the asteroids

around the perimeter of the circle to a teammate with a better shot at a moon. If a moon gets hit with an asteroid, the player trades positions with the thrower who scored the hit.

Objective

The members of the galactic forces try to hit moon players in the center of the circle with a foam-ball asteroid. The human moons hide behind the big activity ball, or sun, to avoid being hit.

Additional Equipment

Players use as many as three foam balls.

Safety Tips

This game is very safe if foam balls are used for asteroids. It may become a bit more hectic if more than three foam balls are introduced into play at a time.

Lead-Ins

- Ball Crawl
- Group Stretches
- Planet Pass

Developmental Skills

- Primary skills include cooperation and throwing and catching.
- Secondary skills include rapid response and coordination.

Duration of Game

Play this game for 5 to 10 minutes.

When to Play

This game can generate lots of activity and excitement. Since it tires the players out, Eclipse fits well near the end of a session.

Follow-Ups

- Ball Surfing
- Bumper Ball

Variations

The moon team can turn the tables by launching the giant sun out at the galactic forces. Only one asteroid is used in this variation. The moons try to roll the renegade sun toward the unprotected players at the edge of the circle. Players on the perimeter of the circle can protect themselves by using the foam-ball asteroid as a cosmic shield. The galactic players should throw or pass the foam ball to the teammate they think is most likely to get hit by the large ball. The moons can shift the orbit of the large sun whenever they like so that it moves toward an undefended member of the galactic-force team.

Teaching Tips

Throwers don't always have to aim the asteroids directly at the moons. Players on the outside of the solar system can pass asteroids around the perimeter to teammates who have a better shot at an exposed moon. This aspect of the game is a great way to teach your players teamwork.

Orbit

· · · · · ·

Orbit is an expression of the age-old conflict between the feet and the hands. For some reason, feet like to kick the ball out of the circle into unknown space, while hands prefer to contain the ball in the familiar territory of the circle.

To create the feet team, 6 to 8 players take off their shoes and lie down on their backs with their heads together, as if they are in the center of a human star. Players in stocking feet usually keep the big activity ball cleaner than those who play wearing shoes. Players on the feet team should also interlock arms with their neighbors. The hands team is comprised of about 15 people who stand in a circle around the feet team, just out of range. Call out for the members of the feet team to put their legs and feet over their heads, then introduce the ball into the center of the circle.

The feet team's goal is to kick the ball into orbit over the heads and hands of the other team. They start kicking their legs in the air, as if they were forming whimsical images of anatomical, undulating flowers in a Busby Berkeley musical number. Of course, they don't have to use the synchronized movements of a coordinated group of

horizontal Rockettes. They can also kick the big activity ball randomly and independently.

The hands team tries to keep the ball in the circle by bouncing it off the other team's feet. If the feet team kicks the ball outside of the circle, they score a point. The hands team scores a point if they manage to keep the ball in the circle for 30 seconds.

Objective

Players on the hands team try to maintain control of the big activity ball. Players on the feet team try to kick the big activity ball out of the circle.

Additional Equipment

None

Safety Tips

Make sure that the members of the feet team keep their heads on the ground. Players who lift up their heads may inadvertently hit someone in the head when they lie down again. They should be able to see well enough while looking straight up with their heads flat on the ground.

Also, make sure players on the feet team kick the ball up and over the heads of the other team's members, not sideways towards their bodies. The ball is more likely to stay up in the air if the hands players stay close enough to the feet team so that the ball can't come down between the two teams. This distance also prevents the feet team from kicking the ball straight at any of the members of the hands team. Of course, you should remind the players on the hands team to stand far enough away so that they don't get kicked by a member of the feet team.

Finally, remind players on the hands team that their goal is to keep the ball moving over the feet team. They should not try to stuff the ball down onto the other team's feet.

Lead-Ins

- Rolling Pin
- Ball Surfing
- Bumper Ball

Developmental Skills

- Primary skills include cooperation and coordination.
- Secondary skills include strength.

Duration of Game

Members of the feet team can get very tired, so each round should only last 30 seconds. A game lasting 5 to 10 minutes should give everyone a chance to play on both teams.

When to Play

Don't start out with this game, but position it early in the session so that the players have enough energy to participate.

Follow-Ups
- Big Bocce
- Sizable Shot Put

Variations
Eliminate the hands team and group players into teams of three. Each team takes turns kicking the ball as far as they can in a lower-body version of Sizable Shot Put. Two assistants toss the ball to each three-person team.

Teaching Tips
Orbit explores the wonder and fun of a big activity ball but provides enough structure to keep the game safe. Because leg muscles are much bigger and stronger than arm muscles, when the members of the feet team work together, they can coordinate a group kick that sends the ball soaring. If you're playing Orbit indoors, make sure the room has a high ceiling.

Parachute Ball

If you have access to a parachute, you can combine it with a big activity ball to make a truly fantastic game. Players stand around the edge of the parachute, keeping a firm grip on the hem. The players must coordinate their movements as a group to make the ball roll around the edge of the parachute. Players raise their edge of the parachute when the ball rolls by them, creating a ramp that sends the ball toward the next player. If the group gets a rhythm going, the ball can move quite quickly.

Objective

Players cooperatively roll the big activity ball around the inside edge of a parachute.

Additional Equipment

Parachute

Safety Tips

Make sure that the giant ball doesn't roll off the parachute or hit any players who may not be paying attention.

Lead-Ins

- Group Stretches
- Group Dribbling

Developmental Skills

- Primary skills include cooperation, keen vision, and rapid response.
- Secondary skills include adaptability, self-control, strength, and communication.

Duration of Game

In Parachute Ball, players usually need a few minutes of practice before they begin to feel successful. Allow at least 5 to 10 minutes to give people enough time to practice, play a few rounds, and then end the game with a feeling of accomplishment.

When to Play

Parachute Ball can be played at any time. However, you should consider when you want to bring out and put away the parachute. It may be a good idea to play at the end of the session, so players can help you pack up the parachute while the ball is deflating.

Follow-Ups

- Ball Surfing
- Bumper Ball

Variations

The group may try to dribble the ball on top of the parachute's center. Players roll up the edge of the parachute so that they are standing two arm's lengths away from the ball. To launch the ball in the air, all players should pull up on the parachute at the same time. To maintain the reverse dribble, players should lower their edge of the parachute as the ball descends and then raise it again.

Teaching Tips

Players feel great when they do this exercise well and frustrated when they can't get the ball to roll around the perimeter of the parachute with gusto. The key to success in this game is timing. Each player must raise the parachute at just the right moment. Tell your players to think of themselves as fans at a sporting event who create a giant wave by raising their arms right after their neighbors do. To keep the ball rolling in a circle, players should wait to raise their section of the parachute until the ball is directly in front of them. If they raise the parachute too soon, the ball will stop rolling, and if they raise the parachute too late, the ball may roll into them.

Semi-Inflated Ball Games

Here are some games to play with the group while you are deflating your activity ball. Incorporating these games into your session may help exuberant players recognize the end of the session and transition into their next activity. Depending on the style, balls vary in the amount of time they take to deflate. Choose the games that match the time needed to deflate your ball.

Ball Surfing

Begin this game when the ball has only half its air. Invite players to come up one at a time and gently roll on and off the ball. If the ball still contains a fair amount of air, players may try falling onto the ball.

Objective

One at a time, players roll over the big activity ball as it deflates.

Additional Equipment

None

Safety Tips

The distance between the ball and the ground should be small enough so that players can roll from the ball safely. When the ball has lost most of its air, it is no longer safe for players to fall down on the ball.

Lead-Ins

- Orbit
- Eclipse

Developmental Skills

- Primary skills include trust.
- Secondary skills include self-control.

Duration of Game

Play until the ball is almost deflated.

When to Play

Play this game at the end of the session.

Follow-Ups

None

Variations

The majority of players lie down on the ground in a line. Ask two to four volunteers to help you roll the deflating ball on top of the players' bodies.

Teaching Tips

Depending on the type of ball you have, it may be difficult to hold your finger in the valve between players. Make sure that you keep the valve near the opening of the ball's outer skin so you don't have to search for it the next time you inflate the ball.

Bumper Ball

Begin this game when the ball has lost half its air. Invite one person to lie down on top of the ball. Other players push various places on the ball to try to raise different parts of the player's body or to bump that person off the ball.

Objective

The group pushes on the deflating activity ball and tries to bounce off a player lying on top.

Additional Equipment

None

Safety Tips

Make sure that players push the ball, not one another.

Lead-Ins

Planet Pass

Developmental Skills

- Primary skills include strength and trust.
- Secondary skills include self-control.

Duration of Game

Continue this game until the ball is deflated.

When to Play

Play this game at the very end of the session.

Follow-Ups

None

Variations

All members of the group push on the ball at the same time to see how high they can make the person lying on top rise up. If the players coordinate their pushing and releasing, they should be able to create a gentle pulse. Participants can also push right after the moment when their neighbors release, as in Parachute Ball, to create a ripple effect around the ball's perimeter.

Teaching Tips

This game is a great example of the way that participants have more fun when they get a little wild. Your job as a leader is to ensure that the players have fun and stay safe. You can help control the energy level of the group by controlling the rate at which the ball deflates. Stand near the ball as it deflates, and hold your finger in the valve to make sure the valve doesn't accidentally close.

Hair Dryer

When you first open the valve of a fully inflated activity ball, the air really gushes out. People just love to stand in front of the escaping air for a quick round of Hair Dryer, in which the air blows their hair around as in a high-fashion photo shoot. There's really no point to this game, but the players enjoy it. Players with long hair can pose for all of the fashion photographers that will surely appear once their tresses start flowing in the wind.

Objective

Players pose in front of the air escaping from the valve of the activity ball as if they are fashion models.

Additional Equipment

None

Safety Tips

None

Lead-Ins

The last game before you start to deflate the big activity ball.

Developmental Skills

- Primary skills include creativity.
- Secondary skills include improvisational acting.

Duration of Game

Players take turns standing in front of the air escaping from the ball until the ball is deflated.

When to Play

Play this game at the very end of the session.

Follow-Ups

None

Variations

Try keeping a light, chiffon scarf aloft in the stream of air escaping from the ball as it deflates.

Teaching Tips

You can help players get into the mood of posing as supermodels with their hair flowing in the wind by playing the role of the high-fashion photographer. Call out words of encouragement: "Yes, beautiful! Great! Smile!"

4

Super Sports

Traditional Games
Played in a Big Way

This chapter highlights 15 modifications of popular sports for play on a gargantuan scale. The original games are sports played all over the world. You will learn to adapt traditional rules and expectations so you and your players can view old sports with fresh eyes. Imagine the fun your players will have as you give these games new life and vibrancy.

Big Billiards

The object of traditional billiards is to control the paths of different billiard balls by hitting them with a cue ball. You move the cue ball by striking it with a cue stick. With a bit of skill, you can use the cue ball to control all the other balls on the table.

In Big Billiards, players aim high-density foam balls, or cue balls, at the giant billiard ball represented by your big activity ball. Players may not touch the billiard ball directly. Instead, they try to make the big activity ball move by throwing foam balls at it.

The group divides into two teams that line up on opposite sides of the field. The big activity ball and foam balls are placed on a line in the center. When the game begins, all players run to the center to collect the foam balls. Players throw foam balls at the big activity ball in an attempt to move it over their opponent's line. Once the round begins, players may occupy any part of the field. They may also go out of bounds to retrieve errant balls. Many teams strategically hoard the foam balls until they have enough to make a group effort to push the big activity ball across the goal line with consecutive blows.

Objective

Players throw foam cue balls at the big billiard ball in an attempt to move it. Their goal is to roll the big activity ball over the other team's goal line.

Additional Equipment

This game works best with lots of high-density foam balls. There are many types of foam balls on the market, but the heavier ones more easily move the big activity ball. Type the words *high-density* and *foam balls* into your favorite Internet search engine for a list of vendors who sell these balls.

Safety Tips

Remind players to throw the foam balls only at the large billiard ball, not at one another.

Lead-Ins

- Towering Team Handball
- Airmail

Developmental Skills

- Primary skills include throwing and catching.
- Secondary skills include cooperation.

Duration of Game

Play this game for 5 to 10 minutes.

When to Play

Play this game once the players have a good sense of the big activity ball's weight. Many of the games at the beginning of chapter 3 are good for this. This game works well toward the end of a play session.

Follow-Ups

- Orbit
- Ball Surfing

Variations

Players can also work together with the foam balls to push the big activity ball through a set course. Time each team's progress from point A to point B with a stopwatch.

Teaching Tips

Players will discover that it is very hard to move a cage ball that is 6 feet (2 m) in diameter by hitting it with foam balls. This game works best with a brand of activity ball that is lighter, such as an Omnikin or a Kin Ball.

This activity effectively demonstrates Sir Isaac Newton's first law of motion: "An object at rest tends to stay at rest. An object in motion tends to stay in motion." Astute players will also discover that it is easier to keep a ball rolling in the same direction than it is to try and reverse the ball. Additionally, it's harder to start a completely stationary ball than it is to maintain slow, steady movement toward the goal.

Big Bocce

In traditional bocce, players try to throw their balls as close as possible to the jack, a smaller ball. One strategy is to throw the bocce ball toward the jack. Players can also throw their ball to knock the other team's bocce ball away from the jack. Bocce has several strategies for knocking the other team's activity balls out of the way. Players may either roll the ball alone or in teams of two.

A standard bocce ball set consists of eight balls, four for each team, and one jack. If you are lucky enough to have eight big activity balls, then your adaptation of the game will be fairly straightforward. Use a foam ball for the jack. If you have only one big activity ball, each player should place a marker to indicate the ball's position after a shot, and then pass the Big Bocce ball on to the next player.

Objective

Players try to roll the big activity ball as close as possible to the jack. The player who rolls the ball closest wins.

Additional Equipment

Foam ball

Safety Tips

None

Lead-Ins

- Shoot the Diameters
- Gigantic Miniature Golf

Developmental Skills

- Primary skills include strength.
- Secondary skills include keen vision.

Duration of Game

Allow 5 to 10 minutes or more for a good game of Big Bocce.

When to Play

Big Bocce can be played at the beginning, middle, or end of a play session.

Follow-Ups

- Orbit
- Mega Rugby

Variations

If they have only one big activity ball, teams should alternate pushing the large ball at the jack. The ball is pushed from the position where it landed during the last team's turn, and they score points if they can make the bocce ball touch the jack. Quite a bit of strategy is involved, since near-misses set the other team up for an easy shot.

One player begins the game by tossing the foam ball, or jack, out on the field. Players from the other team then roll the big activity ball toward the jack. They may try to place the ball close to the jack, or they may opt to roll it in a manner that makes the next shot more difficult for the other team. The section on teaching tips offers more strategies. A point is given to the team that makes the big activity ball touch the jack. That team tosses out the jack for the next round.

Continue play for a certain amount of time or until one team scores a set amount of points.

Teaching Tips

While players must always roll the ball in the direction of the jack, they don't always have to try to get the ball close to the jack. Players often use their turn strategically to set up a bad shot for the next team. They can push the ball gently, so it travels very little, or push it forcefully, so it rolls well past the jack.

Big Double Basketball

Traditional basketball features five players on a team, but Big Double Basketball can accommodate far more! Two teams of players form partnerships by pairing up with someone on their team. Partners may legally pass, dribble, or shoot the giant activity ball only when they are acting as a duo. Their goal is to dribble and pass the ball toward the other team's basket, a hula hoop either placed on the ground or suspended above it. Teams score a point when the ball lands in or rolls over the opponent's hoop.

Objective

Move the ball into or over the other team's hoop.

Additional Equipment

2 big hula hoops

Safety Tips

Big Double Basketball uses the same safety rules as standard basketball. Players are not allowed to charge, trip, push, block, or hold their opponents.

Lead-Ins

Group Dribbling

Developmental Skills

- Primary skills include walking and running.
- Secondary skills include cooperation.

Duration of Game

Play this game for 5 to 15 minutes.

When to Play

Introduce this game once players can handle and dribble the big activity ball with a partner.

Follow-Ups

Because this game is strenuous, follow it up with a relaxing session of a game such as Rolling Pin.

Variations

Large, open carts that hold athletic balls or laundry make great above-ground baskets. Please inspect carts for sharp projections that could damage the ball or hurt a player. If you come up with another way to suspend baskets in the air, we would like to hear about it. See the preface for our contact information.

Teaching Tips

Standard basketball players must practice drills to improve their skills. Big Double Basketball players can also benefit from drilling adaptations of standard basketball skills with a partner.

Colossal Cricket

Colossal Cricket is so huge that it requires three wickets instead of the traditional two. Traditional cricket is similar to baseball. Two teams alternate between playing offense and defense. A bowler on the offensive team tries to bowl the ball past the batter on the defensive team and knock over a wicket. The batter protects the wicket by hitting the ball with a bat. Should the batter hit the ball, any member of the offensive team tries to catch it. If the ball lands before an offensive player catches it, a race ensues. The batter tries to run to the other wicket before any of the fielders throw the ball to the wicket.

Line the wickets up in a straight line so there are two pitches, instead of the standard single pitch. In Colossal Cricket, the wickets are placed in this order: bowler's wicket, batter's wicket, and the new wicket (see figure 4.1).

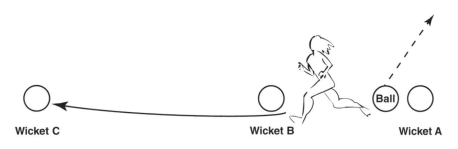

Wicket C   Wicket B   Wicket A

Figure 4.1 "A" represents the bowler's wicket, "B" is the batter's wicket, and "C" is the new, third wicket.

The distance between the bowler's wicket (A in figure 4.1) and the batter's wicket (B in figure 4.1) should be about half as long as the distance between the batter's wicket and the third wicket (C in figure 4.1). You should adjust the distance between the wickets to accommodate your particular group of cricketers after a few innings of play.

The bowler rolls the big activity ball toward the batter's wicket (or B in figure 4.1). For extra oomph, two or more bowlers can roll the ball at the same time. If the ball rolls over the wicket, the defensive team scores an out.

The batter, while defending wicket B, can kick the ball or hit it with a full-body slam. After making contact with the ball, the batter must race to wicket C before the defending team fields the ball and rolls or bounces it over either wicket A or B. If the batter reaches the third wicket before the defending team rolls the ball over another wicket, the offensive team scores a run. If the defenders manage to roll the ball over a wicket before the batter reaches the third wicket, they score an out.

Objective

The bowling team tries to knock over a wicket with the big activity ball. The batting team scores runs when a player strikes the big activity ball and runs to the third wicket before the bowling team achieves its goal.

Additional Equipment

Plastic discs or hula hoops work well as wickets. You can make a more traditional, vertical wicket with two-liter bottles that are half-filled with water.

Safety Tips

The presence of a third wicket makes the game safer and helps maintain the competitive balance between the offensive and defensive sides. The batter should always run away from the path of the rolling ball to avoid being hit.

Lead-Ins

- Shoot the Diameters
- Donut Rolls

Developmental Skills

- Primary skills include running and rapid response.
- Secondary skills include strength.

Duration of Game

Real cricket matches can last for days. Plan on ten to thirty minutes or more for a good game of Colossal Cricket.

When to Play

With seasoned players, Colossal Cricket may be the only game you play for the entire session. If the players are not familiar with a big activity ball, play this game in the middle or at the end of the session.

Follow-Ups

- Ball Surfing
- Ultimate Ultimate

Variations

Depending on the number of players and the amount of time you have, you may choose to end innings after a predetermined number of outs (usually three), or after every player on the offensive side has had a chance to bat.

Teaching Tips

In standard cricket, the batter has the ability to hit the ball quite a distance. The fielders must hustle to get the ball back to a wicket before the batter can run 66 feet (20 m) to the other wicket. The greater distance that the fielders must throw the ball is offset by the fact that they can throw a cricket ball faster than the batter can run. The two factors balance each other out to make an exciting contest.

Colossal Cricket batters will not be able to knock the big activity ball very far. However, the fielders won't be able to roll the ball very quickly either. Experiment with the distances between the three wickets to find a balance between the speed of the runners and the speed of the fielders.

Mega Rugby

In this version of rugby, the offensive team consists of two positions: the carriers and the blockers. Two or more carriers work together to carry the activity ball toward the opponent's goal line in a towel or small blanket. Meanwhile, the defending team throws foam balls at the big activity ball. A towel requires two carriers and a small blanket may need four carriers, with each player holding one edge of the blanket. If the ball rolls off the towel or blanket, it is called a turnover, and the defending team takes possession of the ball. Blockers protect the big activity ball and the carriers by knocking foam balls out of the air with their hands or bodies. They also try to catch the foam balls and throw them away from the big activity ball.

The defensive team consists of only one position, the throwers. Throwers toss the foam balls at the big activity ball, hoping to score a hit. If a foam ball hits the big activity ball, a turnover results, and the teams switch sides. There are no consequences if a foam ball hits a blocker.

Throwers may also aim foam balls at the carriers. If a foam ball strikes a carrier, that player may no longer hold the towel or blanket. The player has two seconds to change roles with a blocker. During those two seconds, a blocker from the same team attempts to replace the carrier and maintain control of the ball. Play continues if the transition is successful. This switch can be risky, so the defensive team can try to force a transition by throwing balls at the carriers.

If the carriers manage to transport the big activity ball into the other team's end zone, the offensive team scores a point, and the teams switch roles.

Objective

Teams of carriers try to transport the big activity ball over the other team's goal line. Blockers protect the big activity ball from the foam balls being hurled by the defensive throwers.

Additional Equipment

- Towels or small blankets
- At least 3 foam balls

Safety Tips

Unlike standard rugby, this is a noncontact sport. Players on opposite teams should maintain a distance of at least one arm's length.

Lead-Ins

Big Volley

Developmental Skills

- Primary skills include throwing and catching and rapid response.
- Secondary skills include running.

Duration of Game

Play this game for at least 10 minutes. Once players understand the rules and the strategy, they can play Mega Rugby for the entire session.

When to Play

Play this game during the middle of a play session or at the end. Players should have some experience with the big activity ball in another game before trying Mega Rugby.

Follow-Ups

Airmail

Variations

Each offensive player may carry the large ball only once per possession. This gives the defensive players a slight edge. If the defense targets each successive carrier, there will be no blockers left who are eligible to become carriers. The next strike of a carrier results in an automatic turnover.

Teaching Tips

This game involves lots of cooperation and strategy. Good blockers are essential to the forward movement of the big activity ball. The carriers must also work together to keep the ball from rolling off the towel. Defensive players don't always have to throw a foam ball at the big activity ball or a carrier. They may choose to pass a foam ball to a teammate who is better positioned to score a hit.

Crab Soccer

This classic game is so well-known that we almost forgot to include it in the book.

In Crab Soccer, two teams vie for control of the ball and attempt to score goals, just as in standard soccer (or football). Players assume the position of crabs by lying on the ground and supporting themselves to rise up on their hands and feet. Their chests and bellies should face the ceiling or sky. Crabs move the ball by kicking or nudging it with one foot.

Objective

Players try to roll the big activity ball over the other team's goal line while maintaining the crab position.

Additional Equipment

None

Safety Tips

The playing field must be safe for people's hands. Crab Soccer should be played either indoors on a clean, wooden floor or outside on an extremely well-manicured lawn.

Lead-Ins

Orbit

Developmental Skills

- Primary skills include rapid response and coordination.
- Secondary skills include endurance.

Duration of Game

Many groups enjoy playing this game for 10 minutes or more.

When to Play

Play this game toward the middle of a play session or at the end.

Follow-Ups

Planet Pass

Variations

A popular variation of Crab Soccer involves four teams. Teams line up along each side of a square, facing in. Place the big activity ball in the center of the square and assign a number to players on each team. Each team has a number one, a number two, a number three, and so on. Call out one or more numbers. The players whose numbers have been called crab walk to the center of the square and try to kick the ball over another line. Players remaining on the side lines may use their feet to defend their line from the ball. These stationary crabs may not leave the lines. If a ball crosses a team's line, that team is awarded a point. The object of the game is to have as few points as possible.

Teaching Tips

You should referee this game rather than play. Remain standing for the best view and mobility.

Big Baseball

Because all the positions are doubled in Big Baseball, your participants may feel like they're playing for the Minnesota Twins, a professional U.S. baseball team. Each team will have two pitchers, two catchers, two shortstops, two batters, and so on.

Four bases are placed in the traditional diamond configuration for Big Baseball. You can vary the distance between the pitchers' mound and home plate, as well as between the bases, to accommodate the size, strength, and ability level of the players in your group.

The pitchers put the big activity ball into play by rolling or bouncing it toward home plate. The batters stand on either side of home plate and simultaneously swing their backsides and hips at the ball. After the hit, both batters run to first base together. Runners try to advance around the bases together while the ball is in play during successive hits. If one of a pair of runners is tagged with the ball, both runners are declared out, and must leave the field. Runners are rolled out when the fielders roll the ball over a base before they reach it.

Objective

Players work in pairs in a large-scale version of baseball. Teams score points by advancing pairs of runners around the four bases.

Additional Equipment

5 hula hoops or plastic discs to serve as large bases

Safety Tips

Choose a big activity ball that is light enough and small enough for the players to safely handle. A ball with a diameter of approximately 4 feet (1.2 m) works well for many players.

Lead-Ins

Hip Check

Developmental Skills

- Primary skills include cooperation.
- Secondary skills include running.

Duration of Game

Games rarely go beyond nine innings. An inning usually lasts for six outs, three outs per team; unless you'd like to change the tradition.

When to Play

A riveting game of Big Baseball could last an entire play session.

Follow-Ups

Conclude with a game that places all of the players on the same team, such as Planet Pass or Rolling Pin.

Variations

Play groups often modify the rules of baseball. Your players may already be familiar with variations such as closing positions in the outfield, using invisible runners, or playing with fewer than three bases. One variation eliminates the need to tag the players out with the ball. Instead, fielders roll the ball back toward home plate. If the ball crosses the plate before the runners reach first base, they are out. This variation eliminates the congestion on first base that occurs when the players and ball arrive at the same time.

Teaching Tips

People have such a strong association between baseball and umpires that you should assume the role with gusto. Practice gesturing grandly as you gruffly shout, "You're out!" or "Safe!"

Towering Team Handball

Unlike traditional team handball, this variation has two goalkeepers and two balls. Players try to throw a foam ball with a diameter of 6 to 8 inches (15-20 cm) into the goal area. The two goalkeepers use the large activity ball to block any attempts at scoring.

The offensive team scores a point whenever one of the players throws the foam ball into the goal. This team also scores a point if the defending goalkeepers use their bodies to block the foam ball. However, the offensive players may not throw the foam ball directly at either of the goalkeepers.

Objective

Players attempt to throw the small foam ball into the other team's goal area.

Additional Equipment

- Foam ball
- 2 goal areas

Safety Tips

None

Lead-Ins

- Eclipse
- Colossal Bowling

Developmental Skills

- Primary skills include rapid response and throwing and catching.
- Secondary skills include cooperation.

Duration of Game

10 to 30 minutes

When to Play

This game is best played in the middle or at the end of the play session.

Follow-Ups

- Airmail
- Big Bocce

Variations

Many people associate this variation of team handball with miniature golf, especially with the golf hole that features a windmill. Two players dribble the big activity ball in place. The dribblers may vary their tempo, but the ball must rise up above their waists each time. The other players take turns trying to throw foam balls underneath the big activity ball. Any player who rolls a ball underneath the big activity ball scores a point.

Teaching Tips

If you only have one big activity ball, play the game on a half-court instead of a full court. Both teams attack the same goal and take turns providing goalkeepers for defense.

Adjust the size of the goal area to match the goalkeepers' skill with the big activity ball.

Big Volley

Try a round of Big Volley if you have access to a strong net that can handle a humongous ball. Many of the rules are the same as standard volleyball, except that more than one player can make contact with the ball at a time. Also, as long as the ball doesn't touch the ground, players may hit the ball more than three times before sending it back over the net.

In this game, the weight of the ball is more important than the size. Imagine one player standing under a ball that is descending from a height of 8 or 10 feet (2.5 to 3 m). If the ball is too heavy, it will hit a solitary player with a great amount of force. Use a lighter ball for maximum safety. If you don't have a lighter ball, consider another game.

Objective

Players attempt to pass the big activity ball over the net and prevent it from touching the ground.

Additional Equipment

None

Safety Tips

Use a net that is stable and low and a ball that is fairly light.

Lead-Ins

Titanic Tennis

Developmental Skills

- Primary skills include cooperation and coordination.
- Secondary skills include keen vision.

Duration of Game

Play this game for 5 to 10 minutes.

When to Play

Play this game in the middle of a play session or at the end.

Follow-Ups

Big Bocce

Variations

This variation combines the games of four square and volleyball. Players must let the ball bounce once on their side before they throw it over the net to the other side.

Teaching Tips

The Big Volley net usually tires before the players do. Move on to another game if the net begins showing signs of wear.

Colossal Bowling

Set ten large pins up in a standard, triangular configuration for Colossal Bowling. In this version of bowling, the pins are less likely to knock their neighboring pins down, so they should be set fairly close together. A good formation places the pins close enough together to create a strike when the ball hits the center of the lead pin.

In Colossal Bowling, partners work together to bowl the big activity ball down a makeshift alley toward the pins.

Objective

Players attempt to knock over as many pins as possible with the big activity ball.

Additional Equipment

Use plastic two-liter bottles for bowling pins. Add water or sand to each bottle until you find a weight that matches your group's skill

level. The average group uses pins that weigh between 100 and 200 grams.

Safety Tips

Bowlers must alert all other players before throwing the ball.

Lead-Ins

- Shoot the Diameters
- Big Bocce

Developmental Skills

- Primary skills include strength.
- Secondary skills include cooperation.

Duration of Game

The length of the game depends on the numbers of bowlers. It should take less than a minute to reset the pins for each pair of bowlers.

When to Play

Colossal Bowling can be played at the beginning, middle, or end of a play session.

Follow-Ups

Titanic Tennis

Variations

In this version, teams score points by setting the pins rather than bowling the ball. Running speed is more important than accuracy. The team with the fastest reset time wins.

Players from one team throw the ball down the empty alley as fast as they can. Once the ball is in motion, the other team tries to set up as many pins in the path of the ball as they can. The setting team scores a point for every pin that gets knocked down. In this race, setters wait until the last possible moment to gauge the ball's direction before placing the pins. However, the setting team must be careful to avoid the ball. If a setter makes contact with the ball, the setter's team forfeits all the points for that frame.

Teaching Tips

Adapt the length of the bowling alley for the skill level of the group. The distance should present an attainable challenge for your players.

Gigantic Miniature Golf

Although the name of this game might seem as much of an oxymoron as the phrase *jumbo shrimp*, it actually best depicts the proportions of the course. The distances between the tees and greens in this gigantic golf game more closely resembles the dimensions of a miniature golf course than the full-sized fairways of traditional golf.

Create a course using hula hoops as holes. Hula hoops should be far enough away from the tees that players must take multiple strokes to reach the hole. Players move the ball down the fairway by pushing or kicking it. They finish the hole by rolling the ball into the hula hoop.

If they have only one ball, players should take turns making shots. In this case, the group shares a score for the game.

Objective

Each team tries to roll the ball into the hole in as few strokes as possible.

Additional Equipment

- One hula hoop for each hole
- Plastic discs for the tees

Safety Tips

The fairway must be clear before the golfers tee off.

Lead-Ins

- Orbit
- Eclipse

Developmental Skills

- Primary skills include strength.
- Secondary skills include keen vision.

Duration of Game

Each hole should take a couple of minutes. You decide how many holes there are on your course.

When to Play

This is a good game for the beginning or middle of a play session.

Follow-Ups

- Group Dribbling
- Mega Rugby

Variations

This version is more challenging because the ball must remain inside of the hula hoop to be counted. Balls that roll over the hula hoop are treated as rim shots. The golfer must take an additional stroke to sink the ball.

Teaching Tips

An average hole for the course should have a par of three strokes. After a few rounds, you can adapt the distance between the holes and the tees to make the game fun and challenging for your players.

Ultimate Ultimate

One great feature of the game Ultimate Frisbee is that the player holding the disc cannot run. Instead, that person must remain stationary until the disc is passed to a teammate. After making a pass, the player is free to run again. This simple rule forces players to work as a team and eliminates grandstanding from the game. It prohibits stars from running all the way down the field by themselves to score a goal.

A similar rule applies to Ultimate Ultimate. While a player can be in motion while touching the ball, no player can touch the ball twice in a row. For instance, after a player pushes the ball toward the other team's end line, another person must touch the ball before the original player can make contact again. Any player who touches the ball twice in a row forfeits possession for the team.

Teams score goals by rolling the big activity ball past the other team's end line. Teammates can work together to score a goal by passing the ball between players as they progress down the field.

Objective

Players try to roll the big activity ball past the other team's goal line.

Additional Equipment

Plastic discs or cones to mark the goal lines

Safety Tips

Players should not grab, push, clip, or tackle other players.

Lead-Ins

- Planet Pass
- Triple Bounce

Developmental Skills

- Primary skills include running and cooperation.
- Secondary skills include endurance.

Duration of Game

Play this game as long as the participants are having fun.

When to Play

This game works well at any point in the play session. However, players should already be familiar with the big activity ball.

Follow-Ups

Bumper Ball

Variations

Limit how far players can move in the zone version of Ultimate Ultimate. Players distribute themselves evenly across the field. Once the game begins, they are only allowed to move three steps from their initial spots. Players may control the ball in their zone, but must pass the ball to a teammate to move it across the field. In this version, players are allowed to touch the ball multiple times in a row.

Teaching Tips

Ultimate Ultimate helps players learn to work cooperatively with their teammates. This is a great exercise for players who tend to dominate games.

Jumbo Hockey

Anyone who has ever whacked a giant activity ball with a hockey stick or racket knows that the jolt that results when the stick connects with the ball can really sting. For this reason, players partner up and use a towel to scoop up and toss the activity ball in Jumbo Hockey. Players in possession of the ball may toss it either to another pair of teammates or toward the goal.

Of course, players from the other team can try to intercept the ball. If two pairs of players arrive at a stray ball at the same time, possession goes to the team that last controlled the ball.

Objective

Players use a towel to scoop and toss the big activity ball over the other team's goal line.

Additional Equipment

One towel for each pair of players

Safety Tips

Players may not run holding their towels stretched tightly between them. They should hold the towel loosely at or below waist level until they are ready to try to move the large ball.

Lead-Ins

Ginormous Juggling

Developmental Skills

- Primary skills include cooperation.
- Secondary skills include strength.

Duration of Game

This game can last the entire session.

When to Play

After a brief warm-up, Jumbo Hockey can be played for the majority of the session.

Follow-Ups

Big Billiards

Variations

Since players have all of those towels handy, why don't they incorporate them into a race? Everybody is on the same team. The object is to roll the big activity ball from point A to point B down a path of towels lying end to end on the ground.

All players start by holding their towels at the beginning, or point A. When the leader says go, players start placing their towels on the ground to create a path for the ball. Two players roll the big activity ball over the towel path. Once the ball rolls over a towel, players can pick it up and move it to a point farther down the terry-cloth path. Track the group's progress with a stopwatch and challenge them to set new records.

Teaching Tips

The length of play time will vary according to the size and energy level of your group.

Titanic Tennis

Titanic Tennis doesn't require any type of racket, but it does require lots of teammates to help get the ball over the net! This game is played much like regular tennis, but you can have more than two players on each side. Another difference is that players use their hands to lift and push the ball over the net. Finally, the ball may bounce three times on a side before it must be sent over the net.

Objective

Players try to throw the ball over the net in a way that prevents the other team from returning it.

Additional Equipment

A tennis court or a makeshift net

Safety Tips

Players are not allowed to touch the ball until it has bounced on their side of the court and has lost some of its original force.

Lead-Ins

Group Dribbling

Developmental Skills

- Primary skills include cooperation and coordination.
- Secondary skills include strength.

Duration of Game

Play this game for 10 to 20 minutes.

When to Play

Titanic Tennis can be played at any point in the session.

Follow-Ups

Airmail

Variations

Players can also partner up and toss the ball over the net with a large beach towel. Most of the standard rules of tennis apply. Once players catch the ball in their towel, they are not allowed to run until they toss it. Players may allow the ball to bounce more than once before they retrieve it. They may also bounce the ball once on their side of the court before it goes over the net. Players should serve the ball while standing about 6 feet (2 m) away from the net.

Teaching Tips

Even small children can push the ball over the net if they can dribble it first to generate some momentum.

Great Wall Handball

Handball is a classic game that involves hitting a small ball against a wall. In the traditional game, the ball may only bounce once before a player must use either hand to strike the ball so it hits the front wall with no bounce. If the ball bounces twice before a player gets to it or fails to reach the front wall on the fly, the other player wins either the point or the chance to serve the ball. Players must serve the ball to score points.

The main difference between regular handball and Great Wall Handball is that there are more than one or two players on a team. Players may use both hands to push the ball back to the wall. Also, wrist shots are not counted as penalties.

Objective

Players bounce the big activity ball against the wall in a manner that prevents the other team from returning it.

Additional Equipment

None

Safety Tips

The main safety concerns in Great Wall Handball are for the ball and the court, not the players. The wall must be sturdy enough to support the weight of ball, and the playing area must be free of debris that could puncture the ball.

Lead-Ins

Bounce Scotch

Developmental Skills

- Primary skills include coordination.
- Secondary skills include rapid response.

Duration of Game

Play this game for 5 to 10 minutes.

When to Play

If players already have experience with a large activity ball, this game may be played at any time.

Follow-Ups

100-Meter Roll

Variations

If you have a wall and playing area that extends for 30 feet (9 m) or more, you can modify this game into a race. Players take turns racing from one end of the wall to the other while bouncing the ball against the wall (see figure 4.2). Use a stopwatch to time the players and see which team can navigate the great wall fastest.

Teaching Tips

The game becomes less fun if there are too many players. Pay attention to the group's interest level and change to a different game if players begin to get bored.

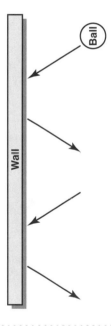

Figure 4.2   Players take turns racing while bouncing the ball against the wall.

5

Humongous Playground Games

Large-Scale Versions of Favorite
Childhood Activities

Playground games are different from sports because playground games are informal and spontaneous and have flexible rules. Because these games don't have official rules, players act as their own referees. Although playground games are sometimes chaotic, they can require as much skill and discipline as the most challenging sports.

The big activity ball fits well with the games that kids play on the playground without adult guidance or intervention. A surprising number of these games are played all around the world with slightly different rules and names. Because players already know and enjoy playground games, you don't have to spend a lot of time explaining new rules. They will probably want to play variations with the big activity ball over and over again.

Wacky Wall Ball

Wacky Wall Ball is a game for two players. If the group is larger than two, players count off to create a fixed order.

1. The first player bounces the big activity ball so that it bounces off the ground once and then hits the wall.

2. After the ball rebounds off the wall, the next player runs to catch the ball before the second bounce. Player 2 then bounces the ball back toward the wall.

3. The third player in line runs up to catch the ball, and so on. The same rule applies to each player: the ball may only bounce once between catches and hits.

As in golf, the player who has the fewest points at the end of Wacky Wall Ball wins. Players may receive penalty points if they fail to catch the ball after the first bounce or if they can't make the ball hit the wall with one bounce. They must race to the wall before someone else retrieves the ball and sends it to the wall. If the player reaches the wall first, no points are awarded and play resumes. If the ball reaches the wall first, the player receives a point.

The play area in front of the wall should be about 30 feet (9 m) deep and 45 feet (14 m) wide. Players stand behind a throw line located 15 feet (4.5 m) from the wall to serve or return the ball. Adjust this distance after a few rounds to match the skill level of the group. Beginners may play without a throw line until they master the basic skills.

Objective

Players take turns catching the big activity ball as it rebounds off the wall and bouncing it toward the wall again. The ball may legally bounce on the ground only once between catches and hits. More bounces may result in penalty points. The winner is the player with the fewest points at the end.

Additional Equipment

- A high, sturdy, smooth, and windowless wall
- Chalk to mark the playing area and throw line

Safety Tips

In the race to determine penalty points, players should bounce the ball toward a point on the wall away from the path of the runner.

Lead-Ins

Two-Minute Hoop Bounce

Developmental Skills

- ● Primary skills include throwing and catching.
- ● Secondary skills include running.

Duration of Game

Good playground games can last the duration of the session. Play for 10 minutes with a small group (3 players) and up to 30 minutes with a larger group (12 players).

When to Play

Wacky Wall Ball can easily take up a whole period. It's best as a final game, when there are at least ten minutes left in the play period.

Follow-Ups

Big Volley

Variations

The winner in this modification is the player with the most points rather than the fewest. Players have a chance to score points when someone else makes a mistake. Mistakes still result in a race to the wall, but points are awarded to the player who retrieves the ball after a failed catch or throws it back to the wall with one bounce. If the runner beats the ball to the wall, no points are awarded and play continues. This version motivates players to pay attention while they wait their turn with the ball.

In another version of Wacky Wall Ball, the group divides into two teams that alternate bouncing the ball against the wall.

Teaching Tips

Referees often have a difficult time judging who reaches the wall first in a racing situation. Players learn more when they are empowered to make fair judgments themselves. If players are becoming crowded when they compete to retrieve a missed ball, you should switch to a game that accommodates a larger group.

Extreme Jacks

Everything you know about playing jacks holds true in Extreme Jacks. The big differences are that Extreme Jacks is played with a very large ball, a small parachute, and five badminton birdies.

Five players hold the edge of a small parachute. They start the game by putting the badminton birdies (jacks) on top of the parachute, then pulling on the edges with a sudden jerk that tosses the birdies up and off the parachute. After the parachute descends, the players roll the ball on top of the parachute, and the game gets really interesting.

The players snap the parachute tight again, which this time tosses the ball up in the air, and the race begins. A player must pick up one jack and throw it onto the parachute before the ball hits. Players snap the parachute for the second round, which tosses the ball and the first

jack upward. Four players try to keep the first jack in the parachute while the fifth player grabs the second jack. Play continues until the team has retrieved all five jacks.

If the game becomes too easy, players can try to pick up two jacks at a time. If they make a mistake, they forfeit their turn to the next team of five. Here are some examples of common mistakes:

- A previously caught jack escapes from the parachute.
- The ball falls off the parachute as it descends.
- A player fails to pick up a jack before the ball hits.
- A player picks up the wrong amount of jacks.

The team that plays the most rounds without making a mistake receives a round of applause from the group.

Objective

Players toss the big activity ball with a small parachute or towel. One player tries to collect the jacks and throw them onto the parachute before the big activity ball lands.

Additional Equipment

- A small parachute or large towel
- 5 badminton birdies (If you don't have badminton birdies, substitute any item that is light, easy to pick up, and doesn't roll.)

Safety Tips

As the players become more advanced, they may choose to move as a unit with the parachute to catch the ball. Individual players may also briefly break away from the parachute to pick up a jack. Players may not run, but may take brisk, walking steps.

Lead-Ins

Parachute Ball

Developmental Skills

- Primary skills include cooperation and rapid response.
- Secondary skills include coordination.

Duration of Game

Play this game for 5 to 10 minutes.

When to Play

Play this game at the beginning or end of a session.

Follow-Ups

Ginormous Juggling

Variations

The traditional game of jacks has many variations. Players may add more birdies or let the large ball bounce once or twice on top of a slack parachute before tightening the parachute to catch the ball.

Teaching Tips

As with all games in which there are a series of steps, players tend to get impatient, trying to rush on to the next level before they have mastered the first. Encourage the players to practice various components of the game by breaking down the steps, and simplifying the challenge. "Let's see if we can play with just two jacks." until they've demonstrated enough mastery to try the "real" game.

Players use a lot of different skills in this game. They must communicate and work together to throw the ball high, to keep the jacks in the parachute, and to move as a group to retrieve additional jacks. Given all that, the most exciting challenge lies in making up new tricks.

Eight Square

Although it isn't twice as big as four square, Eight Square can be twice as fun. This game actually has nine squares, and one big activity ball.

Players use sidewalk chalk to divide each of the sections of a four-square court into two different zones. The court should look something like figure 5.1.

Four players begin the game by standing in each of the smaller squares (see squares with letters in figure 5.1). The home position for each player is the outer, smaller square. A player may only leave home and venture into the larger section of the square to bounce the ball. After bouncing the ball, players must return to the smaller square. They may spend approximately three seconds in the outer

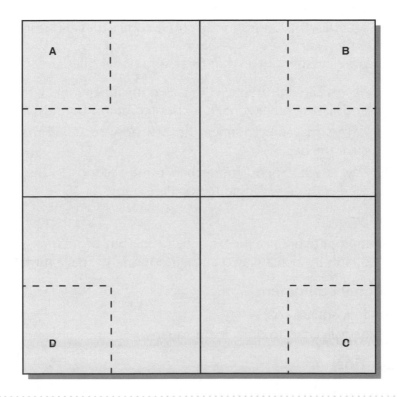

Figure 5.1 Players stand in the smaller squares.

zone. Other players wait to join the game until a square becomes vacant.

Most of the standard rules of four square apply. Players must send the ball over to one of the other three squares if it comes into their section. If the ball bounces twice in a square, the player is out. Players also go out if they don't manage to cleanly return the ball to one of the other three zones. Balls that land on the line are considered out of bounds.

A player who is out moves to the end of the line and the first person in line steps into square D. A player on the court moves up a square if her letter is lower than the vacant square: D moves to C, C moves to B, B moves to A. If the player in square D goes out, the first person in line moves into square D and the players in the other squares maintain their positions.

In Eight Square, a player's luck may change suddenly. No one ever technically wins the game, but the person who manages to occupy square A the longest receives the admiration and respect of the other players.

The game of Eight Square has three additional rules:

1. Players can only bounce the ball in the inner zone. If the ball lands in the outer zone, it is counted out of bounds.
2. Players may only bounce the ball upward. They may not spike the ball.
3. Players who spend more than three seconds in the outer zone without touching the ball are out.

Objective

Players attempt to bounce the big activity ball into any of three opponents' squares in such a way that their opponents make mistakes.

Additional Equipment

- A four-square court
- Sidewalk chalk to draw extra squares

Safety Tips

For younger players, this game works best with an activity ball that has a diameter of 40 inches (1 m) or less.

Lead-Ins

Flip Your Giant Lid

Developmental Skills

- Primary skills include coordination and rapid response.
- Secondary skills include keen vision.

Duration of Game

Games can be as short as 10 minutes and as long as the entire session.

When to Play

This game is best played near the end of the session.

Follow-Ups

Bounce Scotch

Variations

Players can keep score for a competitive version of the game. Only the server, the player in the A square, can score. The server gets a point every time another player misses. Other variations increase or decrease the size of the squares, limit the number of times the server can bounce the ball, or place two players in each square to work as a team.

Teaching Tips

You may want to take an active role in refereeing this game, especially when players start arguing about whether or not the ball was in bounds. However, you can serve your players better by acting as coach and encouraging the players to resolve the problem on their own. You may also help them by pointing out successful strategies.

With a large group, it's better to have several games going simultaneously than to have players waiting in long lines for their turn. Eight players per court are ideal. The ball should always be bounced, not thrown, because it is much easier and safer to bounce a big activity ball. Eight Square stresses agility and coordination over strength.

Flip Your Giant Lid

Flip your lid is a simple game that two participants usually play on a sidewalk with a penny or a popsicle stick and a rubber ball. The game is also known as hit the stick or hit the penny. Flip Your Giant Lid substitutes a big activity ball for the rubber ball and a plastic disc for the penny.

Players use sidewalk chalk to draw three parallel lines about 15 feet (4.5 m) apart. The plastic disc is placed on the middle of the center line. Players stand behind the outer lines and try to hit the lid with the ball. It's as simple as that. Players score 1 point if they hit the lid and 2 points if they flip the lid; hence, the name of the game. Since players are using a big activity ball, they are allowed to throw the ball so it bounces once before it hits the lid.

Objective

Players score points by hitting or flipping a plastic disc with the big activity ball. The winner is the player or team with the highest score at the end of the game.

Additional Equipment

- A plastic disc
- Sidewalk chalk to mark the lines

Safety Tips

None

Lead-Ins

Ping Pong Ball and a Fish Bowl

Developmental Skills

- Primary skills include throwing and catching.
- Secondary skills include rapid response.

Duration of Game

Play this game for 5 to 20 minutes.

When to Play

This game is appropriate between any two large-group activities.

Follow-Ups

Follow this game with one that focuses on accuracy, such as Small-Ball Ricochet.

Variations

- At least 3 people play standing in a circle.
- Players aim at several targets that are each worth a different number of points.
- Two players stand at each end and loft the ball toward the lid as a team.

Teaching Tips

If players have trouble hitting the lid, move the end lines closer. If a large group of players is divided into pairs, they should stand facing each other in two widely spaced, parallel lines.

Bounce Scotch

Imagine a game of hopscotch where the big activity ball replaces the hopper, and you have the game of Bounce Scotch. Two teammates stand on either side of the hopscotch court and work together to bounce the ball through the various squares, avoiding any square that contains a potsie, or marker. Neither the players nor the ball may touch a line at any time. Depending on the configuration of the court, players attempt to navigate themselves and the ball around the court. Players are allowed to jump over squares.

In the classic version of Bounce Scotch, players may bounce the ball only once per square. If the strict version of the game is too challenging, players may be allowed to step on lines or to bounce the ball twice per square.

Any hopscotch pattern may be used. No adjustments to the standard courts are necessary if players use a smaller activity ball. If they wish to play with a really large activity ball, they should make the squares a bit larger to accommodate the ball. The court patterns in figure 5.2 should get you started. You are encouraged to modify any courses to meet your needs.

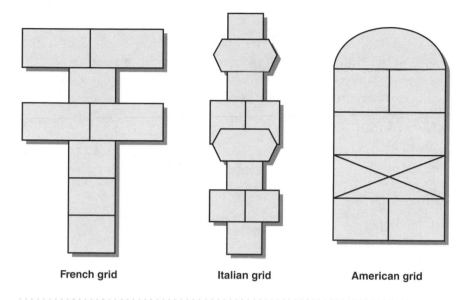

| French grid | Italian grid | American grid |

Figure 5.2 Various hopscotch court configurations.

Objective

Pairs of players try to bounce the big activity ball around a hopscotch court.

Additional Equipment

- One potsie (marker) for each pair of players. Frequently used markers are keys and stones. We don't recommend using cell phones as markers.
- Chalk or masking tape to mark the courts

Safety Tips

None

Lead-Ins

Flip Your Giant Lid

Developmental Skills

- Primary skills include cooperation and coordination.
- Secondary skills include communication and problem solving.

Duration of Game

You should allow at least 10 minutes to play this game, but it can easily last an entire session. If players wish to continue a game past the end of a session, they can leave the potsies on the court and return to the game in the next session.

When to Play

Bounce Scotch can be played as a warm-up before a big game, between two games, or as a cool-down after another game.

Follow-Ups

Bounce Rope

Variations

Partners can alternate bouncing the ball between them instead of working to bounce the ball through the squares together. In this version, teammates stand on opposite sides of the hopscotch court as they move the ball through the various stations.

Teaching Tips

There should be no more than three pairs of players per hopscotch court. If the group is large, teams of players can set up courts around the gym or playground using masking tape or chalk. Players should allow enough room between each court so that the big activity balls don't wander into someone else's game.

Bounce Rope

Bounce Rope is just like jump rope, except that the big activity ball, along with two bouncers, goes over and under a swinging rope. If you squint your eyes, the two games may even begin to look the same.

Four players are needed to begin: two to turn the rope, or turners, and two to bounce the ball, or bouncers. In the beginning, the turners make a big, smooth arc with the rope. The rope must be high enough so the ball can easily fit through and slow enough so that the bouncers can get the timing right. As the bouncers get better at maneuvering the ball, the turners may turn the rope faster, resulting in a shallower arc.

The bouncers stand on opposite sides of the ball and bounce the ball between them. Participants who are waiting to play should stand near a turner. Kids seem to naturally know when to change places during traditional jump-rope games. The same type of general consensus applies to Bounce Rope. Advanced players will be able to

figure out how to enter and exit the game. Bouncers can alternate their positions with other players so that the big activity ball is continually handled by a pair of new players. Players can chant any of the standard jump rope rhymes during the game.

Objective

Players try to cooperatively bounce the big activity ball in various jump-rope patterns.

Additional Equipment

1 long rope for each team of turners

Safety Tips

Turners should maintain a firm yet light grip on the rope, so that if the ball hits the rope or a bouncer, it flies out of their hands rather than yanking them to another part of the playing area. People waiting to play should stand near the turners and away from the bouncers. If more than one game is going on at the same time, players should allow lots of room between games.

Lead-Ins

Flip Your Giant Lid

Developmental Skills

- Primary skills include cooperation and throwing and catching.
- Secondary skills include rapid response.

Duration of Game

This game can be as short as 10 minutes or as long as the entire session.

When to Play

Bounce Rope is a good game to play near the end of the session, or during extended times of low exertion.

Follow-Ups

Eight Square

Variations

As they get better, the bouncers can introduce all kinds of impressive tricks. They can see if they can turn around, or turn around and touch the ground between bounces. Turners may also try Big Double Dutch, in which they turn two ropes simultaneously.

Teaching Tips

Because this is a skill-based game, it will take a while for players to develop competence. Most players will need to be reminded to slow down. The best way to do this is to introduce simple rhymes, chants, or songs to control the tempo.

Wallies
● ● ● ● ● ● ● ●

This version of the basketball game, horse, uses a smooth, windowless wall instead of a basket. Players stand in a line. The first player throws the ball so it bounces once against the ground and then hits the wall. The second player catches the ball, either on the fly or after one bounce, and then tries to hit the same place on the wall as the previous player. Again, the ball may only bounce once between the player and the wall. The next player in line has the same goal and the same rules.

At the beginning of the game, the group picks a word. Wallies is the game's namesake, but variations like chicken, donkey, horse, spot, or pig also work. Players who don't succeed, either because they miss the ball or hit a different spot on the wall, are assigned a letter from the word. Players who receive enough letters to spell the chosen word are out. The winner is the last player standing.

Objective

Players try to bounce the big activity ball so that it hits a wall on the same spot as the previous player's hit. Unsuccessful players receive a letter from the word *wallies*. The first person with enough mistakes to spell the word is out.

Additional Equipment

Play on a smooth surface in front of a smooth and sturdy wall.

Safety Tips

Make sure players always face the wall.

Lead-Ins

Honkin' Big Discus

Developmental Skills

- Primary skills include throwing and catching and rapid response.
- Secondary skills include keen vision.

Duration of Game

Play this game for 5 or 10 minutes.

When to Play

Wallies can be played at any time during a session.

Follow-Ups

Wacky Wall Ball

Variations

You can play a progressive version of Wallies by marking different targets on the wall with masking tape or chalk. Players must progress through the course of targets with successive turns. Vary the height, size, and distance from one target to the next to really challenge your players.

Teaching Tips

Players should bounce the ball against the wall, rather than throw it. However, pairs of players may throw the ball against the wall.

6

Big Athletic Games

Large Track-and-Field Events

For most people, the term *athletic contest* conjures up a classic track-and-field competition featuring running, jumping, and throwing events. This chapter presents ideas on how to modify classic track-and-field events to create your own larger-than-life, inflatable athletic contests. The eight activities in this chapter are interesting and fun, and they provide new challenges for your players.

These challenges are not just physical. They also incorporate team-building skills. Provide players with a basic idea for the events, and then allow them to work collaboratively to develop their own specific techniques.

100-Meter Roll

"On your mark! Get set! Roll!" And they're off! Which members of your group will be able to roll the big activity ball 100 meters the fastest?

Long considered the highlight of a track and field meet, the 100-meter dash loses none of its intensity as it morphs into the rotund 100-meter roll. The rules are simple: players roll a big activity ball from the starting line to the finish. Whoever gets there first wins.

If you have more than one ball, you can pit players against each other in a ball-to-ball competition. If you only have one ball, then you should bring out a stopwatch and run some time trials. A fun way to stage this event is to create teams of two players. The pairs roll the ball between them as they dash toward the finish line.

Objective

Players compete to see who can roll the big activity ball over a set distance the fastest.

Additional Equipment

- A big activity ball for each competitor or team, if possible
- A stopwatch to time individual heats, if necessary

Safety Tips

Make sure the track is wide enough so that each roller has a clear, separate lane.

Lead-Ins

- Rolling Relays
- Triple Bounce

Developmental Skills

- Primary skills include running.
- Secondary skills include cooperation.

Duration of Game

The duration of this game depends on the number of contestants. While the actual time spent rolling the ball 100 meters is short, it can take a while to set up for this event.

When to Play

This activity is appropriate at any point in the track-and-field event. The order for these events depends on the level of difficulty for setting up different stations.

Follow-Ups

- Hurdles
- Triple Bounce

Variations

Turn this activity into an obstacle course by placing configurations of hoops on the ground for the players to roll over, or patterns of cones for them to roll around.

Teaching Tips

This activity is a great way to teach teamwork as pairs of players roll the ball together.

Hurdles

Transform your 100-Meter Roll course with a set of hurdles. Players bounce the balls down the course, instead of rolling them.

Objective

Players compete to see who can bounce the big activity ball over the hurdles on the track.

Additional Equipment

- Hurdles: Regulation hurdles are great if you have them. You can also make hurdles from one or two large plastic bottles.
- A stopwatch

Safety Tips

Construct hurdles out of items that are safe for both the players and the big activity ball.

Lead-Ins
- 100-Meter Roll
- Triple Bounce

Developmental Skills
- Primary skills include running.
- Secondary skills include cooperation.

Duration of Game
As in the 100-Meter Roll, each heat only takes a few seconds. The total duration of this activity depends on the number of competitors and the amount of time needed to set up and take down the equipment.

When to Play
This contest fits well into any part of a track-and-field event.

Follow-Ups
100-Meter Roll

Variations
A team of 3 players makes for an intricate hurdling event. Teammates alternate acting as the hurdle. One player runs out in front of the ball and crouches down on the ground to become the first hurdle. The other two players bounce the ball over the human hurdle. After the ball clears the human hurdle, that player switches places with one of the two rollers. The player who was tagged runs ahead of the ball to become the second hurdle, and so on. Play continues until all players have taken a turn acting as both a hurdle and a roller. The finish line should be a short distance beyond the third human hurdle.

Teaching Tips
Use plastic discs to mark spots for the human hurdles.

Rolling Relays

In Rolling Relays, teams of four work together to roll the big activity ball from the starting line to the finish line. Teammates take turns rolling the big activity ball over each other. Two rollers move the ball forward two body lengths at a time over two rollees, who lie down to create a human track for the ball.

To begin, all four players position themselves around the activity ball. At your signal, the first two rollees form a line by lying down in front of the ball, feet to head.

The two remaining players, the rollers, roll the big activity ball over the two rollees. Once the ball has rolled over these two players. Then all four players switch positions. The two rollers become the rollees and lie down in front of the ball while the two rollees stand up and become rollers. Players continue switching roles until the big activity ball crosses the finish line.

Objective

Teammates take turns lying down to become the track and rolling the ball over each other.

Additional Equipment

A stopwatch

Safety Tips

Remind the rollees to keep their legs together, their arms at their sides, and their heads down. Remind the rollers to avoid stepping on the rollees as they roll the big activity ball over their teammates.

Lead-Ins

- ● Group Dribbling
- ● Ball Crawl

Developmental Skills

- ● Primary skills include cooperation and rapid response.
- ● Secondary skills include communication and trust.

Duration of Game

The duration of this game depends on the length of the course and the speed at which your players can switch roles. The course should be long enough so every member of the team gets rolled over at least twice, or two lengths per teammate.

When to Play

This contest fits well into any part of a games session with a big activity ball, especially as part of a big activity ball track-and-field event.

Follow-Ups

- ● Broad Bounce
- ● Triple Bounce

Variations

A more competitive version of Rolling Relays pits two rollers against all of the other players. Two rollers try to roll the big activity ball over the course as fast as they can. Players from other teams lie down in front of the ball to act as speed bumps, trying to impede the ball's progress with their prone bodies. Remind the speed bumps to keep their heads down and their hands and feet at their sides.

Teaching Tips

One of the fun parts of Rolling Relays is the hectic amount of activity that accompanies each transition between rollees and rollers. In the excitement, the ball may make some inadvertent forward progress toward the finish line. Make sure you are equally lax or strict with each team during these transitions.

High Throw

How high can the players toss a huge ball? Will a promising young athlete come up with an entirely new technique that will revolutionize the sport, just as Dick Fosbury showed the world a better high jump with the Fosbury flop? Set up a high bar and find out.

There are several different ways to stage this event. Individual players can make solo attempts, or teams of 2 or 3 players may compete together. Should the attempts be static or dynamic? May athletes use a runway to build up some speed for a dynamic high throw, or should they throw from a standing position? Try both methods to see if the contestants modify their strategies for the different versions. Regardless of the chosen method, the High Throw with a big activity ball is always a fun track-and-field event.

Objective

Players compete to see who can throw the big activity ball the highest.

Additional Equipment

You will need a method to mark the heights of the attempts, such as a high bar. If you don't have a high bar, try resting a broom between the rungs of two stepladders. This method allows you to vary the height of the high bar quickly and easily. A net strung between two volleyball poles also makes a decent high bar. You can also moisten the ball with a wet towel before the athletes toss the ball against a smooth, concrete wall. The ball leaves a damp spot on the wall, and you can measure the distance between the spot and the ground to find the height of the toss.

Safety Tips

Bystanders must stand at a distance to avoid being hit by a falling ball, crossbeam, or support.

Lead-Ins

- Hurdles
- Broad Bounce

Developmental Skills

- Primary skills include strength.
- Secondary skills include coordination.

Duration of Game

The duration of this game depends on the number of competitors. Each actual attempt lasts only a few seconds. However, competitors should be allowed a set amount of time to plan out their strategies before each attempt.

When to Play

This game is appropriate for any part of a larger track-and-field event. You should consider the time and effort needed to set up and take down your improvised high bar.

Follow-Ups

- Honkin' Big Discus
- Sizable Shot Put

Variations

Players bounce the ball on the ground forcefully, so that it clears the high bar after the bounce.

Teaching Tips

When players work together in teams, High Throw becomes a problem-solving activity as well as a test of physical prowess. Give the teams some time to adapt their strategies for lofting the ball.

Broad Bounce

In this version of the broad jump, athletes try to launch the ball as far as possible in one bounce.

Contestants must release the ball from a standing position. They are not allowed to run or jump. Competitors may choose to either loft the ball high or throw it toward the ground. Measure the distance from the launch line to the second time the ball touches the ground.

Objective

Players compete to see who can bounce the big activity ball the farthest from a stationary position. The distance is measured at the second bounce.

Additional Equipment

If you don't want to record individual distances, set down a marker for each attempt. The player whose marker is farthest from the line wins.

- Tape measure to record the distances
- Items such as poker chips or flying discs to serve as markers

Safety Tips

Players should stand clear of the landing pit.

Lead-Ins

High Throw

Developmental Skills

- Primary skills include strength.
- Secondary skills include throwing and catching.

Duration of Game

The time for each attempt is very short, but it may take a while to set up for this activity.

When to Play

This contest fits well into any part of a track-and-field event.

Follow-Ups

Triple Bounce

Variations

Pairs of players work together to launch the ball as far as they can. You can also measure from the first time the ball touches the ground, as in the traditional broad jump. This variation shifts the focus of the game from strategy to strength.

Teaching Tips

If you give the contestants freedom to experiment, the event becomes somewhat scientific. Let them try out various strategies and modify their techniques as they go along.

Triple Bounce

Players may take a running start to build up momentum for the Triple Bounce. Contestants try to bounce the ball the greatest distance down the field. The ball is allowed to bounce three times before the distance is marked.

Players may run beside or behind the ball while they bounce it down the runway, and may continue to run beside the ball and nudge it forward during the next two bounces. Players may not carry the ball at any point.

Objective

Players compete to see who can bounce the big activity ball the farthest while running. The distance is measured at the fourth bounce.

Additional Equipment

- Tape measure
- Markers

Safety Tips

Other players and observers should stay away from the pit.

Lead-Ins

Broad Bounce

Developmental Skills

- Primary skills include coordination and strength.
- Secondary skills include running.

Duration of Game

Players are allowed one minute for each triple bounce. You'll also need some time to set up and take down the equipment.

When to Play

This contest fits well into any part of a track-and-field event.

Follow-Ups

Honkin' Big Discus

Variations

This can also be an event for a series of pairs of players. Partners may try running beside the ball for the entire attempt or starting at different points along the course. In the latter case, the first partner passes the ball to the second partner, who completes the final two bounces.

Teaching Tips

This event is not just a contest of strength. Contestants will achieve better results by watching and learning from previous attempts. Can they achieve a greater distance by lofting the ball up or by dribbling the ball down? Let your players experiment with various methods to see which work the best for them.

Honkin' Big Discus

Who can loft the ball the farthest? Set up the arena, give everyone a chance to make a mighty heave, and find out. Will players try an underhand scoop in the manner of Wilt Chamberlain shooting a free throw? Is an Atlas-style pose, with the ball hoisted on the upper back and shoulders, the most effective posture for launching the ball? Let the games begin! Empirical results are only a Honkin' Big Discus throw away.

Honkin' Big Discus has surprisingly few rules. Results are not as important as the opportunity to explore different techniques. Players experiment with methods for launching the big activity ball and get feedback on their ideas. They can use their feet, hands, or a combination of both to launch the ball. Once players lift the ball off of the ground, they must commit to a method. Distance is measured from where the players are standing to wherever the ball lands, even if the ball inadvertently slips out of the players' hands.

Objective

Players choose a method for launching the big activity ball. The distance is measured at the first bounce.

Additional Equipment

- Tape measure
- Markers

Safety Tips

Players should stand clear of the landing pit.

Lead-Ins

Triple Bounce

Developmental Skills

- Primary skills include strength.
- Secondary skills include coordination.

Duration of Game

Each team gets approximately one minute to prepare and release the discus.

When to Play

Honkin' Big Discus is appropriate for any point in the play session.

Follow-Ups

- Sizable Shot Put
- Rolling Relays

Variations

Players can try rolling the ball for distance, instead of throwing it. They may also throw the ball in teams of two or three.

Teaching Tips

Let contestants experiment with different techniques before you give them tips or guidelines.

Sizable Shot Put

In this game, players lie down on the ground and use their feet to launch the ball as far as possible. Teams of three each take turns launching the ball. Two players maneuver the ball into the initial position for the third player who is lying on the ground. Each team gets three attempts, and each member should take a turn as the launcher.

Objective

Teams compete to see who can launch the big activity ball farthest using their feet. The distance is measured at the first bounce.

Additional Equipment

Tape measure or markers

Safety Tips

Players should stand clear of the landing pit.

Lead-Ins

Honkin' Big Discus

Developmental Skills

- Primary skills include strength and cooperation.
- Secondary skills include problem solving.

Duration of Game

You might impose a time limit of 10 or 20 seconds for each attempt. Part of the fun of this activity is seeing how players position themselves to launch the ball while under pressure.

When to Play

This game can be played at any point in the session.

Follow-Ups

High Throw

Variations

Pairs of players launch the ball together. In teams of three, this means that only one player can position the ball for the launchers. If you have teams of four, two players can be positioners, and two can be launchers.

Teaching Tips

Players can use Sizable Shot Put as a problem-solving game. Let the participants discover how to best address the challenge. You could create a science lesson that compares the results between Sizable Shot Put and Honkin' Big Discus. In your group, are leg muscles or arm muscles stronger?

Ginormous World-Record Challenges

· · · · · · · · · · · · · · · · ·

Using Your Big Activity Ball to Earn a Place in History

Whether or not you make it into the *Guinness Book of World Records*, the art of creating a challenging feat and performing it to the best of your abilities is enormously satisfying. When your world-record attempts include big activity balls, the potential for fun becomes ginormous!

Designing a World-Record Challenge

It's remarkably easy to design a world-record challenge. For example, suppose the challenge was to establish the world record for the greatest number of balls that three people can hold off the ground for at least a minute. You can immediately change at least five parameters to make the challenge your own:

1. The number of big activity balls
2. The size of the activity balls
3. The number of people
4. The distance between the ground and the activity balls
5. The length of time the activity balls are held

You can also give your participants additional challenges to make the world-record attempt more unique. Suggest that participants do the following while holding up the activity balls:

- Stand on one foot
- Place one hand on someone else's head
- Close their eyes
- Remain silent
- Walk in a circle
- Hold one hand behind their backs
- Dress up as a football player

Be creative! Feel free to take suggestions from the group.

World-record attempts can be truly wacky. Here are a few unusual Guinness records that were set at London's Flora Marathon in 2007:

- Fastest person to run the marathon dressed as Elvis
- Fastest female to run the marathon wearing a superhero costume
- Most linked runners to complete a marathon
- Longest scarf knitted while running a marathon
- Fastest person to run the marathon wearing a fireman's uniform

Almost anything can be a wonderful resource for a new world-record challenge. Many world-record challenges from this chapter draw inspiration from the cooperative games from chapter 3. Many of these games are suggested as lead-ins for this chapter's activities.

Players don't need to beat established world records to have fun with these activities. Though they may enjoy competing and testing their skills against a global standard, they will gain more from creating their own unique challenges.

Players who design successful world-record challenges have realistic expectations. Most failures result from expectations that are either too low or too high. Help players create appropriate challenges that strike the balance between fantasy and reality.

General Equipment for Creating World Records

These basic items will help you shatter previous world records and create brand new ones:

- Camera or video camera for documentation; a stopwatch to mark your record-setting times; and a clipboard, poster boards, flip charts, or a computer that can be used to keep a written record
- At least 1 big activity ball between 4 and 5 feet (about 1.5 m) in diameter
- Several smaller activity balls between 2 and 3 feet (about 1 m) in diameter

The following optional items will help set an official mood for your world-record attempt:

- Tape measures
- Viewing stands
- Umpire chairs
- Team t-shirts

The Process of Creating World-Record Challenges

The following seven ideas will help you create a new world record:

1. *Select the challenge.* Players select their goal from a list of world-record challenges or come up with an idea on their own. Selecting the challenge is part of the group process and should take about 15 minutes. If players discuss the challenge for too long, they will lose momentum. If they spend too little time in discussion, they may overlook some important decisions. Emphasize uniqueness, creativity, humor, agility, coordination, teamwork, and safety.

2. *Practice.* Participants spend 15 minutes developing competencies for their challenge, evaluating their attempts, and then trying to beat their own records. It is always wise to master the basic task before trying to see how fast you can perform it. They should also discuss strategies for success.

3. *Perform.* Players next perform their selected challenge for a judge, a panel of judges, or a group. Witnesses should document the event with cameras. This portion of the event should last about five minutes.

4. *Record.* Once the players have made their best attempt, the judges should note it on a list of records. Ideally, the judges will post this list where everyone can see to provide a sense of accomplishment and closure. Other groups can try to beat the record, the record-setters can try to beat their own record, or people can just create newer and wackier world records.

5. *Repeat.* If the participants enjoy the event, you can conduct world-record attempts regularly, holding them once a week, once a month, or perhaps once or twice a year for the greater community. When world-record attempts become an ongoing tradition, participants become more focused on and dedicated to the events.

6. *Time the event.* Each challenge should last about 20 minutes: 15 minutes to practice and 5 minutes for the official attempt, including witnessing, timing, measuring, and recording.

7. *Plan when to play.* Although these activities work well immediately after a cooperative game, they can be appropriate at any time.

Ginormous Juggling

Juggling, especially with really large balls, is a perfect task for a world-record attempt. Successfully throwing and catching even one ball is spectacular when the ball is enormous. Of course, the higher you throw the balls, the more likely you will be to set a world record.

Because players will struggle to throw and catch a big activity ball with their hands, Ginormous Juggling requires a team of players with a parachute. Two teams of four take one moderately big activity ball and two small parachutes or blankets. Their goal is to toss the ball back and forth between parachutes as many times as possible without dropping it. Teams have more success tossing the ball back and forth if they line up as pairs along the sides of the blanket, rather than placing one player on each of the four sides. This configuration keeps players clear of the ball.

Once the groups have practiced throwing the ball back and forth about four times, they should meet to choose their Ginormous Juggling challenge.

Objective

Using two parachutes, two teams of players work cooperatively to toss the big activity ball back and forth as many times as possible.

Additional Equipment

2 small parachutes, blankets, or large towels

Safety Tips

The parachute must be larger than the ball so that the players don't get hit in the head or face as they catch the ball.

Lead-Ins

Parachute Ball

Developmental Skills

- Primary skills include cooperation and strength.
- Secondary skills include endurance.

Follow-Ups

Big Volley

Variations

Here are some modifications for the game:

- Increase the number and variety of the balls
- Encourage players to move during the challenge (rotate around the parachute, rotate around each other)
- Require players to let the ball hit the ground once before catching it in the parachute
- Perform to music
- Try the game with three groups and three parachutes

Other world-record attempts include the longest juggling time, the greatest number of activity balls, the longest juggling time while players close their eyes, or the longest juggling time while players are dressed as caterpillars.

Teaching Tips

Coordination, collaboration, and creativity are all central to the success of this activity. The event can also become competitive. If one team is doing something silly, the other teams will want to do something sillier. If one team is doing something spectacular, the other teams will want to increase their level of spectacularity. You can channel the group's competitive energy by shifting the emphasis from originality to performance. Encouraging players to compete with each other will help them focus their energy and develop their skills. If you wish to diffuse the competition, encourage players to create unique challenges. This will draw out their collaborative skills, their creativity, and their humor.

Group Ball Touch

The concept for this challenge is simple: capture the world record for the greatest number of people simultaneously touching a big activity ball. The area of contact can be as small as a fingertip. The ball can be held on the ground, suspended between participants, or overhead. Get your camera ready and huddle around!

Objective

Players work cooperatively to simultaneously touch the big activity ball.

Additional Equipment

None

Safety Tips

This challenge requires people to stand close together. Use and practice a safety phrase, such as "Back up, please," in case anyone feels squished.

Lead-Ins

Group Stretches

Developmental Skills

- Primary skills include cooperation and appropriate touch
- Secondary skills include problem solving.

Follow-Ups

Rolling Pin

Variations

- How many people can touch a big activity ball with various parts of their bodies like their elbows, heads, shoulders, feet, and backsides?
- How many people can touch a slightly smaller ball?
- How many different body parts can one group use to touch the ball?
- How many people can keep a big activity ball from touching the ground while turning?

Teaching Tips

Leaders may want to observe this activity rather than participate. They should be able to take in the whole scene and gauge the group's comfort level.

Big Kid Pile-Up

Kids of a certain age love to pile on top of each other. This challenge helps your players explore this impulse and keeps you out of the fray!

Objective

Players work cooperatively to hang from the big activity ball at the same time.

Additional Equipment

A split-second stopwatch

Safety Tips

A few players should act as spotters to make sure no one gets squished. The group should also practice and use a safety phrase, such as "Back up, please," in case someone gets uncomfortable.

Lead-Ins

- Group Stretches
- Ball Crawl

Developmental Skills

- Primary skills include cooperation and balancing.
- Secondary skills include problem solving.

Follow-Ups

Mega Rugby

Variations

Another challenge is the *fewest* number of players who can hang from the ball for three seconds.

Teaching Tips

The ball should be slightly deflated for this activity. Players should first practice piling on the ball with their feet on the ground. At your signal, players should simultaneously lift their feet for a second. If they do well, players may try hanging for a longer period of time. Before you know it, the *Guinness Book of World Records* representative will be giving you a call.

Small-Ball Ricochet

Bouncing a small ball off a big activity ball is easy. After all, the activity ball is hard to miss. However, catching the small ball after it bounces off the big activity ball is much more challenging.

The foam ball must be caught on the fly. Any player can catch the foam ball. The player who catches the foam ball must throw it back at the activity ball within the next two or three seconds.

Objective

Players work cooperatively to bounce a foam ball off the big activity ball and catch it as many times as possible.

Additional Equipment

- A trash can or laundry basket for the big activity ball's base
- At least 1 high-density foam ball

Safety Tips

None

Lead-Ins

Group Dribbling

Developmental Skills

- Primary skills include throwing and catching and keen vision.
- Secondary skills include rapid response.

Follow-Ups

Planet Pass

Variations

Players can place the activity ball against a wall or in a corner, rather than in the center of the playing area. Once players master this challenge, they can start throwing more small balls against the big activity ball. Their new challenge would be to create a world record for the greatest number of successful catches with the new number of balls.

Teaching Tips

Unless players throw the small ball at precisely the right spot, it is almost impossible to predict the direction of the small ball during the rebound. For success in this challenge, players should spread out around the activity ball so they are ready to catch the foam ball, no matter where it flies.

Use an object like a trash can as a stand to elevate the activity ball. This allows players to aim more easily at the ball's circumference. A stand also keeps the activity ball from rolling away when it is hit.

Nine-Person Ball Pass

This challenge is based on the classic over and under relay. However, there are a few differences. The competitors use a big activity ball to challenge their own abilities, rather than racing against another team.

Objective

Players work cooperatively to pass a big activity ball down the line in as little time as possible. Players alternate passing the ball either over their heads or between their legs.

Additional Equipment

A stopwatch

Safety Tips

The activity ball should be no taller than the players' waists. Players should stand far enough apart so that they can travel with the ball as they attempt to climb over it.

Lead-Ins

Ball Crawl

Developmental Skills

- Primary skills include coordination and strength.
- Secondary skills include rapid response.

Follow-Ups

Crab Soccer

Variations

- Increase the size of a ball.
- Players stand in a circle instead of a line.
- Players pass two balls of different colors and sizes from opposite ends of the line.

Teaching Tips

Players should practice strategies for getting the ball through the line or circle quickly. Wait to time the race until players have developed a good strategy for keeping the line intact as they pass the ball. Many players assume they must face forward. In fact, they may turn around to help the player behind them.

Two-Minute Hoop Bounce

In the game of box ball, players bounce a rubber ball into a sidewalk square and over to an opponent without hitting any lines in the sidewalk. The challenge shifts when the game is played with a big activity ball and a hula hoop. Instead of competing for points, players work together to set a world record.

Place the hula hoop in the middle of a group of 2 to 6 players. One player serves by bouncing the big activity ball into the hula hoop, and over to another player. The ball must cleanly bounce into the hoop, without touching the sides.

The receiving player bounces the ball to another player. The ball must always bounce once in the hula hoop as it travels between players. The ball doesn't have to move among the players in any set order, although players may be able to keep the volley going longer if they have a path in mind. Play starts over if the ball bounces more than once between players or touches the hula hoop.

Objective

Players work cooperatively to bounce a big activity ball in and out of a hula hoop as many times as possible in two minutes.

Additional Equipment

Hula hoop

Safety Tips

None

Lead-Ins

Hurdles

Developmental Skills

- Primary skills include cooperation and rapid response.
- Secondary skills include coordination and communication.

Follow-Ups

Eight Square

Variations

Groups that are dedicated to teamwork may try the game with two hula hoops and two balls. Players should determine a fixed order for passing the ball in this variation. The timing of this game is the biggest challenge, since players must work together to keep the two big activity balls from colliding.

Teaching Tips

Adjust the distance between the players and the hoop to accommodate the size of the ball, and the ability level of the players. Experiment to find the best positions before players attempt a world record.

Super Spin

This game is like spinning a very large top. Since no lifting is required, you can use your largest ball. Gather as many players as possible around the ball. At your signal, players set the ball spinning with a mighty push.

Objective

Players work cooperatively to push the big activity ball so that it spins for as long as possible.

Additional Equipment

A stopwatch

Safety Tips

None

Lead-Ins

Orbit

Developmental Skills

- Primary skills include strength.
- Secondary skills include cooperation.

Follow-Ups

Group Dribbling

Variations

You can vary the number of spinners or the number of balls. See how many balls the group can spin simultaneously or how long a small group of players can spin the ball.

Teaching Tips

This game requires at least two players standing on either side of the ball. If players cannot see each other over the ball, encourage them to develop some verbal signals.

Here is a list of undeveloped world-record ideas:

- Small Ball Balance: How long can you keep a smaller ball on a big activity ball without touching it?
- Big Ball Carry: How fast can two people run a set distance while carrying a big activity ball with tennis racquets? You can change the number of people, the distance, the size of the ball, the number of balls, and even the number of rackets for different world-record attempts.
- Balance Run: How fast can six people run a set distance holding a big activity ball on their backs? Can they run 100 yards (91 m) without dropping the ball?
- Big Ball Kick: How far can players send an activity ball using only their feet?
- Highest Single Bounce
- Biggest Wall Bounce
- Longest Ball Ride: How far can the players safely carry the big activity ball with one of the players on top of the ball?

8

Very Big Midways

Giant Carnival Games

"Step right up. Step right up. That's right, I'm talking to you. Try your luck. Test your skills. Win a round of applause and the undying adulation of your peers. It's the carnival of giants, and you're about to be taken for a ride into some very big fun!" This chapter features two kinds of midway activities: games of luck and skill and carnival rides.

The challenge in games of luck and skill is to find the right level of difficulty for your players. Good midway games are easy enough that they can be won, but not so easy that every player becomes a winner. If the game is too challenging, the players will be frustrated. If it is not challenging enough, the players will get bored.

Another reason that these activities are so much fun is that the challenges are accessible. These games help your players learn the art of setting an achievable goal that is central to all physical training. Again, your job as leader is to seek balance. If the challenges are too easy, players will never develop their skills or strength, and if they are too difficult, players will eventually give up.

These games are true to the spirit of carnival games in that players need both luck and skill to win. These games emphasize skills but they also encourage kids to play, to participate, and to use their bodies. Players should remember that their goal is fun, not winning. This spirit of teamwork may inspire your school, organization, or community to host a whole carnival of big activity ball games.

Did you ever think your big activity ball could be used by multiple players as a piece of playground equipment? The rides section of this chapter shows you how your players can hang from, bounce off, and go for a ride on the big activity ball.

Prizes of little worth also enhance the carnival spirit. Search the back of your equipment closet for dead tennis balls, mortally wounded golf balls, and flightless badminton birdies. The games are fun enough that players may not need prizes, but most game leaders have closets full of worthless treasures on hand. If you're tempted to offer better prizes, follow in the tradition of most carnivals and give away inexpensive prizes.

Recruit a group of carnies, or players who help organize, referee, and generally facilitate the games, to test each game before you officially open it. If a game is impossible to win, it's no fun. Encourage the carnies to make up their own variations and to modify the game to accommodate space and equipment restrictions, as well as the skill level of the players. Each game and ride is structured to be easily adapted. You can also use these activities to help your players learn to create meaningful challenges. The ultimate criterion is fun.

Games

After your players experience the games in this chapter, they will probably create lots of new games with a big activity ball for the midway theme. Feel free to experiment! Inventing new games is fun and exciting for kids of all ages and those who are kids at heart.

Poof-a-Ball

If you've ever watched the television show *World's Funniest Videos*, you've probably seen this dangerous but tempting scenario involving a large, somewhat deflated raft in a lake or swimming pool. One person is lying on a raft until someone else jumps onto it and shoots the first person off into space.

Poof-a-Ball is a kinder, gentler version of that scenario that incorporates a big activity ball, a dense foam ball, and a target (trash can or carton). A foam ball replaces the person lying on the raft, and a big activity ball that is partially inflated replaces the raft. Instead of one jumper, this game features two or even three launchers.

The target is placed about 10 feet (3 m) away from the big activity ball. Conduct a few trial runs before you determine the exact placement of the target. Once you get a sense of how far your players can launch the foam ball, you can adjust the distance between the activity ball and the target. The competitors smush the foam ball into the big activity ball, trying to aim the smaller ball at the target. When they are ready, players should push simultaneously and strategically on the sides of the big activity ball. Their goal is to launch the foam ball into the target.

Objective
Players use a big activity ball that is partially deflated to launch a smaller ball into the target.

Additional Equipment
- 1 high-density foam ball, approximately 6 to 8 inches (15 to 20 cm) in diameter
- Trash can or box to use as the target

Safety Tips
It's highly likely that the small ball will miss the target and fly off in an unexpected direction. This scenario is completely safe if you use a foam ball, but you should still let bystanders know when a ball is about to be launched.

Lead-Ins
Any game involving a partially deflated ball would be appropriate.

Developmental Skills
- Primary skills include cooperation.
- Secondary skills include strength.

Duration of Game
Allow players two minutes for each turn.

When to Play

Poof-a-Ball is especially appropriate when you're already in the process of deflating a big activity ball.

Follow-Ups

Any carnival or world-record game would be an appropriate follow-up.

Variations

The target could be a basketball hoop or a volleyball net.

Teaching Tips

Give players at least one practice shot so they get a feel for the game. The carnies could offer a demonstration before the game begins.

Ping Pong Ball and a Fish Bowl

This is a large-scale version of the classic midway game in which players throw a Ping Pong ball into a fish bowl. In this version, you won't need to purchase any fish food! Place some hula hoops on the ground, leaving plenty of space between each hoop. Use a rope to designate a zone away from the hoops where the players will stand. Their goal is to heave or roll the ball into one of the hoops.

Objective

Players try to throw the big activity ball into one of the hula hoops that is lying on the ground.

Additional Equipment

- 3 to 9 hula hoops
- Some rope to make a throwing line

Safety Tips

Players must stay out of the active zone, or the area between the throwers and the hoops.

Lead-Ins

Almost any game would be an appropriate lead-in.

Developmental Skills

- Primary skills include strength and keen vision.
- Secondary skills include cooperation and self-control.

Duration of Game

Allow approximately one minute for each player (or team of players) to retrieve, aim, toss, and mark the score.

When to Play

This is a good game to play at the beginning of a session. This game also works well played in the middle. Be sure to have the hula hoops and boundary marker on hand and ready to set up.

Follow-Ups

If you clear the hula hoops away, you have an open area suitable for almost any midway game. You could also play a more active game such as Giant Soccer.

Variations

Depending on the size of the ball, players can form teams of two, three, or even four. Teams must figure out how to collectively lift and throw the ball. Cooperation, teamwork, and timing become paramount when groups of players try to throw the ball both accurately and in unison.

Teaching Tips

As game leader, you set the tone for the importance of winning. The players will quickly adapt their expectations to how strictly you keep track of scores.

Roll-a-Row

You can roll a big activity ball, probably even hard enough so that it rolls right over objects in its path like hula hoops. You can probably even roll the ball so that it stops right inside that hula hoop, if you concentrated hard enough. But can you roll a ball through three hula hoops lying in a row? Can you make the ball stop in the second hoop? Do you think you can roll balls so that they land in a row of three? Well, then step right up. The game's on!

Place nine hula hoops on the ground in the formation of a giant tic-tac-toe board. Designate a rolling line a set distance away from the board with a length of rope or two markers.

Each player or team of players is allowed three tries to roll the balls into the hula hoops on the board and try for a winning score as in tic-tac-toe. When the balls in the hoops form a complete line of three, either vertically, horizontally, or diagonally, the team has scored a win.

On each round, a player tries to roll the big activity ball so it stops inside one of the hoops. If you are fortunate enough to have three

big activity balls, you can leave the ball in the hoop as the player rolls the second ball. If you only have one activity ball, you should place a marker in the hoop where the ball landed and roll the ball back to the second player.

Depending on how many players you have, you can allow each contestant to have four or more rolls to try to get three in a row.

Objective

Players try to get a winning tic-tac-toe score by rolling the big activity ball into a 3-by-3 grid of hula hoops. Each team is allowed three rolls.

Additional Equipment

Use nine hula hoops to set up the tic-tac-toe board. If you don't have that many hula hoops, construct a tic-tac-toe board by taping squares on the floor.

Safety Tips

Players should exercise caution when more than one game is going on at the same time. Balls that are pushed forcefully may roll into another group. This scenario will not hurt anyone, but you might consider posting a few immovable objects at critical points on the borders of the rolling alley.

Lead-Ins

Gigantic Miniature Golf

Developmental Skills

- Primary skills include keen vision.
- Secondary skills include coordination.

Duration of Game

Each player will need three to five minutes.

When to Play

Play Roll-a-Row either before or after a more active game.

Follow-Ups

Ping Pong Ball and a Fish Bowl would be a good follow-up to this game because rolling and throwing are very different skills, and what you learn doing one activity, you have to unlearn doing the other. Roll-a-Row is different because you roll the ball, and the ball must stay inside the hoop, and therein lies the challenge and most significant difference.

Variations

Vary the number and arrangement of the hula hoops. You could use six hula hoops to form a triangle, and the players' goal would be to get just two balls in a row. You could also place five hula hoops in a pattern like the five on a die. The players' object would be to get one ball in the center and two on any of the sides.

Teaching Tips

It may take a while to master the game of Roll-a-Row, so each player should get at least one practice shot before the game begins. You may allow more practice shots for more difficult configurations. This game can also be easily extended into a Giant Miniature Golf course.

Rock-and-Roll-Off

Many carnival midways feature the ladder climb, a diagonal ladder made of rope that is attached at both ends with swivels. The challenge is to climb the ladder to the end and ring the bell to win a prize. In some versions you carry a ball to the top and drop the ball in a basket. Because the ladder can swivel, the slightest imbalance causes the rope ladder to swing so you are underneath the ladder instead of on top of it. The trick to succeeding at this challenge is always to place your hands and feet on the section of rope between the rungs, never directly on the rungs.

Rock-and-Roll-Off simulates the rope ladder game. Players stand in two lines facing each other, then lie down on their backs and place their feet in the air. There should be enough space between the two lines of feet to support the activity ball. The players' goal is to walk the ball up the track of human feet and place it in a basket at the end of the line.

Two carnies heft the ball onto the first pair of feet. Being very careful to avoid people's heads, the carnies walk along with the ball and help it stay centered on the track of feet. The carnies act as spotters in this game, not rollers. They can gently push and guide the ball back onto the path, but they shouldn't roll the ball up the ramp of feet. The challenge of advancing the ball up the ramp of feet belongs to the players. Get the ball in the basket, and win a collective Kewpie doll!

Objective

Players lie on their backs in two lines with their feet in the air. Players work cooperatively to pass the big activity ball with their feet up the line of people and place it in the basket.

Additional Equipment

A trash can or large box to use as the basket

Safety Tips

Contestants should be aware that the ball may roll off the track of feet and toward a player's head. They should be ready to deflect the ball with their arms and hands if this happens.

Lead-Ins

Hoop on the Ball

Developmental Skills

- Primary skills include cooperation.
- Secondary skills include coordination.

Duration of Game

A typical round lasts three to five minutes. Because this game involves quite a bit of teamwork, let the teams have a few tries to get the ball in the basket.

When to Play

This game works well at the end of a session. The feeling of accomplishment that your players experience when they finally get the ball in the basket makes this a great final game. The game can also be played in the middle of a session.

Follow-Ups
Ball Surfing

Variations
Players divide into two teams of four. Players lie down on their backs, with their feet in the center, to form two small islands of feet. The two teams try to pass the ball back and forth with their feet.

Teaching Tips
The carnies can help the team by providing verbal feedback.

Hoop on the Ball (Giant Ring Toss)

"Step a little closer. Put your feet right here on the line. Take a hoop, any hoop will do. See that big activity ball? Well, all you have to do is get your hoop to land on the ball and stay there. Don't be shy. Try a little wrist action as you fling the hoop. Know what I mean? Release that hoop just as you would throw a flying disc."

Players take turns trying to throw a hula hoop toward the big activity ball. The hoop must either completely encircle the ball or balance on the ball without touching the ground.

Objective

Players try to throw a hula hoop so that it lands on top of or around the big activity ball.

Additional Equipment

Hoops and balls of different sizes

Safety Tips

Bystanders should stand clear of flying hula hoops.

Lead-Ins

- Big Double Basketball
- Wacky Wall Ball
- Any game involving hand-eye coordination

Developmental Skills

- Primary skills include coordination.
- Secondary skills include keen vision.

Duration of Game

Each player may try for two to five minutes.

When to Play

Play either before or after a large-group activity.

Follow-Ups

Follow this game with any of the world-record activities.

Variations

Players may try to throw different objects onto the big activity ball, such as a plastic disc, a hat, a jacket, or even a washcloth.

Teaching Tips

Many factors are critical in determining the fun and appeal of this game: the size of the target balls and objects, the arrangement of the objects, and the distance from the thrower to the target, to name a few. Carnies should test all these factors before they invite others to try their luck. Learning to create a game that is inviting rather than overwhelming is one of the greatest challenges of leading midway games.

Lord of the Very Big Rings

The games that seem the simplest are often the most challenging. Try placing three hula hoops in a straight line on the ground. The object is to bounce a big activity ball over the rings so that it lands inside each ring once. Some may be skeptical, but if the rings are placed just right, it can be done.

Establish a throwing line for the contestants. Players attempt to bounce the big activity ball inside each of the rings without touching any of the sides. Lord of the Very Big Rings can be thought of as an advanced version of Roll-a-Row. In Roll-a-Row, players have three chances to roll the big activity ball into a row of three hoops. In Lord of the Very Big Rings, players get one chance to bounce the big activity ball into and through all three rings.

Objective

Players try to throw the big activity ball so that it bounces once in each of three hula hoops that are on the ground.

Additional Equipment

3 hula hoops

Safety Tips

The boundaries between this game and the other activities should be clearly and visibly marked. Bystanders should stand clear of the ball.

Lead-Ins

- Group Dribbling
- Eight Square

Developmental Skills

- Primary skills include coordination and keen vision.
- Secondary skills include strength.

Duration of Game

Allow two to five minutes for each player.

When to Play

Lord of the Very Big Rings makes a good alternative activity for a small group while the rest of the class is engaged in a larger game. This game really shines when it is included with other midway games.

Follow-Ups

Two–Minute Hoop Bounce

Variations

Set the hoops up in the shape of the letter L. Contestants should work in pairs. One partner stands near the second hoop and tries to redirect the big activity ball into the third hoop as it bounces by.

Teaching Tips

The players who set up the game must try it out before opening it up for general play. Your goal is to help the players understand how to create a good challenge.

Knock 'Em Down

Remember that carnival game where you tried to knock down a pyramid of milk bottles with one throw of the ball? Do you think you could knock down a pyramid of cardboard boxes if you had a ball that was big enough?

Players roll, throw, or bounce the big activity ball so that it knocks over three cardboard boxes.

Objective

Players use the big activity ball to knock down a pile of cardboard boxes.

Safety Tips

The runway must be clear before players put the ball into play.

Additional Equipment

At least 3 empty cardboard boxes

Lead-Ins

Small-Ball Ricochet

Developmental Skills

- Primary skills include throwing and catching.
- Secondary skills include strength.

Duration of Game

Each player is allowed two to three minutes.

When to Play

Play this game after any session in which the players expend a lot of energy. It is also a good featured activity in a session devoted to midway games, world records, or playground games.

Follow-Ups

Follow this game with any activity that involves throwing.

Variations

- Establish more than one throw line and offer a bigger prize for knocking the pyramid down from the greatest distance.
- Reverse the task—players throw a big activity ball at a pyramid of smaller balls.
- Players must alter their manner of throwing. If they have been rolling the ball, they should switch to bouncing it.
- Two players shoot at the same time.

Teaching Tips

Appoint a couple of carnies to restack the pyramid and fetch the ball after each round.

Giant Shooting Gallery

What carnival would be complete without a shooting gallery? This game requires the help of three carnies. One carny takes care of the customers while the other two stand at the back of the booth and roll or bounce the big activity ball back and forth between them.

The shooters throw foam balls at the activity ball. Any shooter who hits a carny with a foam ball loses.

Objective

Shooters try to hit the rolling activity ball with smaller foam balls.

Additional Equipment

At least 6 foam balls

Safety Tips

The two carnies who roll and bounce the ball should stand far enough apart so that they don't get hit by one of the foam balls.

Lead-Ins

Towering Team Handball

Developmental Skills

- Primary skills include throwing and catching and keen vision.
- Secondary skills include coordination.

When to Play

This game can be played any time, and it can easily involve a whole class. You can extend the width of the shooting gallery to the greatest distance that the two carnies can roll the ball back and forth. You could also place lines of shooters on both sides of the big activity ball.

Follow-Ups

Any of the playground games would be appropriate follow-ups.

Variations

Try varying the size and number of the balls used in the gallery. They can range in size from soccer balls to big cage balls. Offer a higher prize to anyone who hits a smaller ball. Allow the rollers to throw the smaller balls back and forth.

Teaching Tips

For success in this event, the number and size of the target balls should match the skill level of the players, the shooting and boundary lines should be clearly defined, and the rollers should coordinate their efforts to keep the big activity ball in motion.

Smack-A-Mole

Invented in 1971 by Aaron Fechter, Whac-A-Mole is a classic carnival and arcade game. Smack-A-Mole recreates that same arcade fun on a gigantic scale.

Two to four players establish a nice steady rhythm by bouncing the big activity ball in one spot. Their efforts are a stationary form of Group Dribbling. The other players in the group take turns trying to bounce or roll a foam ball—the mole in this game—underneath the bouncing activity ball. If a mole scoots safely under the big activity ball, the player that threw it scores a point.

The dribblers are the smackers in this game. Once the game begins, they try to alter the rhythm of the bounces so the big activity ball lands on top of the moles passing underneath. Smackers receive a point for each mole they squish. They must bounce the big activity ball so that the bottom is above their knees at the top of the bounce.

Objective

Smackers try to crush any moles that roll under the big activity ball as it bounces. The other players try to throw or roll a foam ball, or mole, safely under the big activity ball while it is in the air.

Additional Equipment

At least 1 foam ball

Safety Tips

Throwers must stand at least two arm's lengths away from the big activity ball.

Lead-Ins

- Group Dribbling
- Any of the carnival games

Developmental Skills

- Primary skills include throwing and catching and coordination.
- Secondary skills include keen vision and cooperation.

Duration of Game

Smack-A-Mole usually last for 5 to 10 minutes, or until you run out of tokens.

When to Play

This game can be played any time, and can easily involve a whole group.

Follow-Ups

Follow this activity with any of the other carnival games.

Variations

Smackers must bounce the big activity ball along a short course between two rows of mole rollers.

Teaching Tips

Smacking a mole becomes too easy if the smackers don't dribble the big activity ball at least as high as their knees.

Rides

What midway is complete without rides? Big activity balls are great for simulating this favorite midway experience!

Big Bouncer

The Big Bouncer ride requires 8 players and a big activity ball. The players assume one of two roles, a leaner or a bouncer. Each leaner teams up with a bouncer. The leaners form groups of four and prop their backs against a partially deflated activity ball. There should be one leaner balanced on each quadrant of the ball. Bouncers stand a little bit less than two arm's lengths away from their leaners, facing them.

The first pair of partners gets the game going. Holding hands, the bouncer gently pulls the leaner away from the ball a few inches (5 cm), and then lets go. The leaner falls back against the ball. This force on the ball pushes the other leaners up and toward their respective bouncers. The other bouncers pull their leaners up a bit, and then let them fall back against the ball.

This sets up a chain reaction: when one leaner falls back against the ball, the other leaners bounce away. Bouncers can coordinate their efforts by letting their leaners fall back at different times and at different speeds. Their goal is to maintain enough bounce and variety to keep the game fun.

The first round of the game ends after one minute. Players switch roles for the next round.

Objective

Players work with partners and take turns falling backward against the big activity ball.

Additional Equipment

None

Safety Tips

Make sure the leaners don't land too close to one another and knock heads. Bouncers serve as the safety guards for the ride, and should carefully coordinate the movement of their partners.

Lead-Ins

Merry-Go-Round-and-Round

Developmental Skills

- *Leaners*
  - Primary skills include balancing.
  - Secondary skills include trust.
- *Bouncers*
  - Primary skills include strength.
  - Secondary skills include coordination.

Duration of Game

Each round should last one minute. Each game should last at least two rounds so that participants have a chance to play both leaner and bouncer.

When to Play

Big Bouncer incorporates trust and teamwork. It is best to play this game with players who already have some experience and familiarity with the big activity ball.

Follow-Ups

Small-Ball Ricochet

Variations

Leaners number off, one through four. Bouncers alternate their movements so that leaners 1 and 3 fall back against the ball at the same time, followed by leaners 2 and 4. Bouncers can also try to create a wave that bounces players around the ball in turn. What would happen if all four bouncers coordinated their efforts to send all four leaners back against the ball at the same time?

Teaching Tips

Big Bouncer works better if the pairs of players are about the same size. Although it is not critical, Big Bouncer works best when all eight players are roughly the same size.

Merry-Go-Round-and-Round

· · · · · · · · · · · ·

You can think of it as a merry-go-round or as a kid-spinning machine. Either way, your players will think that this game is great fun. As they play, they will exercise their bodies and build their teamwork skills.

Four players, or riders, hold hands across the top of the big ball. The best handhold is the classic, hand-to-wrist firefighter's grip. Players rest their bellies against the ball and lift their feet off the ground.

At this point, two or more ride masters begin to gently rock and spin the ball around. How far can they tip the merry-go-round and still keep the players on the ball as a unit?

Objective

Players grasp hands over the top of the big activity ball and hang off the sides. Ride masters spin the ball around to give the players a ride.

Additional Equipment

You may want to play this game on a mat.

Safety Tips

The ride masters' goal is to give the players a fun ride. They should not tip the ball over so abruptly that the players fall off.

Lead-Ins

Group Stretches is an excellent lead-in for this activity.

Developmental Skills

- *Riders*
  - Primary skills include cooperation.
  - Secondary skills include trust.
- *Ride Masters*
  - Primary skills include cooperation and strength.
  - Secondary skills include endurance.

Duration of Game

Each ride should last one minute.

When to Play

This is a good game for the middle of a session. Participants should have experience with the big activity ball before playing.

Follow-Ups

- Rolling Pin
- Any of the world-record challenges

Variations

The riders can try to spin themselves around by gently pushing off with their feet.

Teaching Tips

Since the safety and fun of this ride depends so much on the ride masters, they should practice spinning and riding on the ball for each other before spinning others. Coach the ride masters as they practice. Invite them to discuss which experiences were fun, what made them feel safe or unsafe, and how they could make the ride more fun.

Tilt-A-World

Just like the Tilt-A-Whirls seen at carnivals and county fairs, a round on the Tilt-A-World gives each rider an unpredictable series of rolls, dips, and spins. The Tilt-A-World version is much slower than its counterpart, however.

Two able spotters are needed for Tilt-A-World. The spotters stand at the sides of the big activity ball, ready to support the lone rider and provide the action. One player jumps towards the top of the ball. The player doesn't have to jump up to the top; she just needs to plaster her body between the equator and the North Pole of the ball. The spotters hold the player against the ball and roll the ball under the rider, so the rider is splayed out on top of the ball.

Both spotters hold the rider against the ball as they slowly roll the ball forward, to either side, and back. Gently roll the ball backward at the end of the ride to let the rider slide off the ball feet first.

Objective

Riders have fun, and spotters gently roll and rock the ball under the rider.

Additional Equipment

None

Safety Tips

The spotters should have a firm grip on the rider. Begin with just slight rolls. With experience the spotters will know how far forward or to the side they can roll the big activity ball under the rider without the rider sliding off. At the end of the ride let the rider slide off the back of the ball so she lands feet first.

Lead-Ins

An active game such as Boulder Roll or Crab Soccer.

Developmental Skills

- Primary skills include trust.
- Secondary skills include communication.

Duration of Game

A thirty-second to one-minute ride allows the rider to experience an initial feeling of novelty and then be able to calm down and enjoy the sensation of being tilted in various directions. The total amount of time for the game depends on how many riders are lining up to have a ride.

When to Play

This game is best played in the middle of a play session. Tilt-A-World is a great chance for the players to catch their breaths after an active game. It is also nice to introduce Tilt-A-World after the players have had a chance to touch and bounce the ball in other games, so they know how strong the ball is.

Follow-Ups

- Orbit
- Planet Pass

Variations

An adventurous player who has already had a comfortable experience of one or more rounds of Tilt-A-World may opt to lie on her back for an additional round. In this version the player backs up to the ball with arms and legs outstretched. The spotters plaster the player's arms and legs against the ball as they roll the ball under the player. The near-upside-down view of the earth, sky, and other players is a treat.

Teaching Tips

Begin slowly and gently. The two spotters will be able to feel how far they can tip the ball and keep the rider from sliding off. As the spotters get more confident they can roll the ball farther. The spotters can also assure the rider that things are under control.

CHAPTER

9

Making a Big Splash

Playing Water Games With a Big Activity Ball

The 10 games in chapter 9 show how a big activity ball can add to your fun in a pool or lake. Some of the games, such as Humongous Water Polo and Marco Ball-O, are adaptations of traditional pool games. Other games are specifically designed for play in the water with a big activity ball. All players should be comfortable wading and swimming in the water to participate in these games.

Use balls for water games without a fabric covering that may absorb water and make the ball unduly heavy. Soft PVC balls are good for pool activities because their skin is strong. If your big activity ball comes with a cover, you can remove it and play with just the bladder. Be aware, though, that playing without the cover makes the ball more vulnerable. In general, the smaller activity balls that people use for personal exercises work well for the games in this chapter. Be sure to rinse any chlorine off the ball when you are finished playing the games.

Humongous Water Polo

Humongous Water Polo is similar to standard water polo in that two teams compete to score goals in a pool. In the big version, any player may touch the ball with both hands.

Players may struggle to swim for the entire duration of the game in deeper water. Depending on the age, size, and ability of your players, you may want to stage the game in shallow water, giving participants the option to wade.

Objective

Players score points by moving the ball to the other team's end wall of the pool. The team with the most points at the end of the game wins.

Additional Equipment

You probably won't have a net large enough to serve as a goal for a big activity ball. If this is the case, designate goal areas on each side of the pool with waterproof tape or life jackets for markers.

Safety Tips

As with all games played in the water, standard water safety concerns are paramount.

Lead-Ins

A good training exercise for this game is for partners dribbling the ball around the pool while using swimming strokes. One player can dribble a Pilates-sized exercise ball by herself. While still possible, larger activity balls may require the help of a partner to dribble.

Developmental Skills

- Primary skills include endurance and rapid response.
- Secondary skills include coordination.

Duration of Game

This game can last as long as the players are having fun. Rounds of play should last five minutes at most. While standard water polo games finish in four periods, feel free to adjust the number of periods for your group.

When to Play

This game could be the sole focus of an entire play session.

Follow-Ups

Follow this game with a pool activity that has less structure.

Variations

Introduce the one-breath rule. Players may only dribble the ball for as long they can hold one breath. After one breath, another teammate must touch the ball before the initial player can make contact again.

Teaching Tips

You should referee from the deck of the pool to get the best overview of all of the players.

Swim-Overs

In this game, players hold the ball underwater long enough for one member of the team to swim cleanly over it. Players must have a great deal of coordination to hold the ball still enough for that length of time. The team that successfully allows a player to swim over the ball with no contact scores a point.

Objective

Players submerge the ball long enough for teammates to swim over it.

Additional Equipment

None

Safety Tips

Standard pool safety rules apply.

Lead-Ins

Swim-Unders

Developmental Skills

- Primary skills include cooperation.
- Secondary skills include problem solving.

Duration of Game

The duration of the game depends on the number of players. There should be a time limit for each attempt. Start with a time limit of 30 seconds for each round, and adjust the amount of time for the needs of your group.

When to Play

This is a good game for the beginning or middle of a session.

Follow-Ups

World-Record Dunking

Variations

Try an aquatic version of Ball Surfing with a big activity ball. As the surfer swims over the partially submerged ball, two team members assist by rolling the ball under the surfer. A line of surfers can successively roll over the ball. Don't forget to let the two players who act as rollers also have a turn as surfers.

Teaching Tips

Big activity balls are very buoyant. The number of players needed to submerge a big activity ball depends on the sizes of the players and the ball. Try this game with a smaller activity ball first, and upgrade to a larger size as your players gain skill and experience. Even a relatively small ball will require the teamwork of an entire group to hold it underwater for any length of time.

Swim-Unders

Two players hold the ball stationary on the surface of the water, a few meters away from the side of the pool. A third player dives from the side of the pool and stays underwater long enough to swim underneath the ball. The diver may not touch any part of the activity ball during the swim.

Once all of the players have had a chance to dive under the ball, move it a bit farther away from the side of the pool for the second round.

Objective

Divers try to extend the underwater portion of their dives to surface on the other side of the big activity ball.

Additional Equipment

None

Safety Tips

Standard pool safety rules apply. Players should dive into the deep end of the pool.

Lead-Ins

Swim-Overs

Developmental Skills

- Primary skills include endurance.
- Secondary skills include strength.

Duration of Game

The length of the game depends on the number of players. Each individual attempt should take under a minute.

When to Play

This game can be played at any time in the session. It's not a great team-building activity, though, so you may want to end a play session with a different game.

Follow-Ups

Water Bomber

Variations

The game can be more competitive if the two swimmers holding the ball are on the opposite team of the diver. In this version, the ball begins much closer to the side of the pool than in regular Swim-Unders. Once the diver is in the air, the swimmers begin moving the ball away from the side of the pool. The diver tries to swim under the ball before running out of breath.

Teaching Tips

This game offers short bursts of activity to individual players. The group spends the majority of its time waiting in line. If you are trying to maintain a high energy level for the group, this game may not be the best choice.

Marco Ball-O

● ● ● ● ● ● ● ● ● ● ● ● ●

This call-and-response game is based on the popular game of Marco Polo, which is played in pools everywhere. In traditional Marco Polo, the person who is It must keep his or her eyes closed. That person tries to ascertain the location of the other players in the pool by the sound of their voices and tag them. When the person who is It calls out the word *Marco,* all of the other players must respond with the word *Polo.*

In Marco Ball-O, there are two teams, the Navy and the pirates. The pirates try to smuggle the ball past the Navy, from one side of the pool to the other.

Navy sailors play with their eyes closed. The pirates are allowed to keep their eyes open as they attempt to keep the contraband ball away from the Navy. When a Navy sailor calls out Marco, one of the pirates must slap the ball loud enough to make an audible response.

Pirates avoid the Navy by swimming with or pushing the ball as silently as possible. The round ends when any Navy sailor touches the ball or when the pirates successfully smuggle the ball across the width of the pool. Teams switch roles for round 2.

Objective

The members of the pirate team try to silently float the big activity ball from one side of the pool to the other in a given amount of time. The length of time depends on the size of the pool and the number of players. Start with one-minute periods and adjust the time accordingly for your situation. The members of the Navy team, who keep their eyes closed, try to touch the big activity ball before it reaches the other side of the pool.

Additional Equipment

None

Safety Tips

Standard pool safety rules apply.

Lead-Ins

Any pool game would work well as a lead-in.

Developmental Skills

- Primary skills include cooperation.
- Secondary skills include communication.

Duration of Game

Play this game for 5 to 10 minutes.

When to Play

This game is appropriate at any point in the play session.

Follow-Ups

Any pool game would be an appropriate follow-up.

Variations

You can make things a little easier for the pirates by setting some limits. Set a one- or two-minute time limit. If the Navy does not find the ball in that time, the pirates score a point. You can also give the Navy a maximum number of times they may call out Marco. If the Navy team uses up its limit of shout-outs before they discover the smuggled ball, the pirates win the round.

In a more goal-oriented version of Marco Ball-O, the pirates try to float the ball silently past the Navy from one side of the pool to the other, but the pirates begin with the ball outside of the pool. After the Navy sailors close their eyes, all of the pirates enter the pool. The pirates also choose one side of the pool for the ball as the starting point. The pirates try to get into the pool with the ball as quietly as possible.

Teaching Tips

Just as in traditional Marco Polo, the number of players is very flexible. As long as there is enough room to maneuver, all of the players in the pool can participate in Marco Ball-O. The ball is a loud and cumbersome object to move around the pool. You can level the playing field and make it easier for the pirates by having more pirates than Navy sailors.

Water Bomber

• • • • • • • • • • • • • •

Water Bomber is a friendly, competitive game between two teams of aerial firefighters. The object is to retrieve the water bomb and deliver it safely to the fire. A water polo ball represents the water dropped by a water bomber to put out a forest fire. The big activity ball temporarily stands for a floating conflagration.

The big activity ball floats in the middle of the pool. Players from both teams tread water around the big activity ball. There are no specific positions in which to tread water, and each team may choose to deploy its members around the big activity ball as it sees fit. Some members may tread water close to the big activity ball, others may choose to be farther away from the big activity ball. One player from each team, the deck hand, stands on the deck beside the pool.

The deck hands take turns launching a water polo ball into the air so that it lands on the big activity ball. The swimmers try to catch the water polo ball after it bounces off the big activity ball. If a swimmer catches the water polo ball before it strikes the water, that team scores a point.

If the water polo ball lands in the water before a player catches it, the game turns into an aquatic version of capture the flag. Any player may pick up the ball and try to swim with it to the edge of the pool. Players on the other team try to tag the player with the ball. If the player with the ball makes it to the edge, that team scores a point. If the player with the ball gets tagged, the team that made the tag scores a point.

The player with the ball may choose to pass it to a teammate if a tag is imminent. This move can be risky, however, since the opposing team may intercept the ball.

Objective

If a player catches the water polo ball before it touches the water, that team scores a point. If the water polo ball touches the water, both teams try to control the ball and escort it safely to the edge of the pool to score a point. The team without possession of the ball can score a point tagging the person with the ball. The team with the most points at the end of the game wins.

Additional Equipment

One water polo ball

Safety Tips

Deck hands should launch the ball at least 10 feet (3 m) in the air.

Lead-Ins

- Swim-Overs
- Swim-Unders

Developmental Skills

- Primary skills include rapid response and coordination.
- Secondary skills include cooperation.

Duration of Game

This game can be played for a set amount of time or until one team reaches 11 points.

When to Play

Play this game toward the middle of the play session.

Follow-Ups

World-Record Dunking

Variations

One team is in the water and the other team is on deck. The players on deck take turns launching the water polo ball so that it lands on the larger ball. The team in the water tries to move the big activity ball away from the water polo ball. The launching team scores a point for each direct hit. The water team scores a point if they prevent a collision between the big activity ball and the water polo ball.

In this variation, a round (inning) lasts for 10 attempts. At the end of the round, the teams change roles and positions.

Teaching Tips

The water polo ball tends to bounce off the big activity ball in an unpredictable fashion. The position of various swimmers can influence the outcome of the game. Let the players learn from experience for the best outcome.

World-Record Dunking

The number of players for this game can be many or few. You'll need a stopwatch or a watch with a second hand. Timing starts when the ball is completely submerged. Note how many seconds your group can keep the big activity ball from bubbling back up to the surface. If your group can easily keep the ball under the water for one full minute, you should consider switching to a larger ball to provide a greater challenge. This game could also fit in chapter 7, Ginormous World Record Challenges, but because the ball is in the water, we included it in this chapter.

Objective

Players work cooperatively to keep the big activity ball submerged under water for as long as possible.

Additional Equipment

Stopwatch

Safety Tips

Standard pool safety rules apply.

Lead-Ins

Swim-Overs

Developmental Skills

- Primary skills include problem solving.
- Secondary skills include cooperation.

Duration of Game

The duration of the game depends on the size of the ball. Usually, a single round of this game is over in seconds.

When to Play

This is a good game for the beginning or end of a play session in the water.

Follow-Ups

Swim-Unders

Variations

What is the fewest number of people who can keep the ball completely submerged for five seconds?

Teaching Tips

Use a relatively small activity ball for this activity. An exercise ball works well.

Life Raft

Imagine you are adrift at sea. Your ship is down at the bottom of the ocean, and the only flotsam left from the voyage is a big activity ball. Can your players situate themselves so the buoyancy of the ball supports all of the survivors? Will the shipwrecked survivors be able to paddle to shore as a group without losing anybody?

Objective

See how many players can cooperatively use the big activity ball to paddle to the edge of the pool.

Additional Equipment

None

Safety Tips

Standard pool safety rules apply.

Lead-Ins

Ships Ahoy

Developmental Skills

- Primary skills include cooperation and problem solving.
- Secondary skills include communication and appropriate touch.

Duration of Game

Give players a few minutes to figure out a group strategy.

When to Play

This game can be played at the beginning, middle, or end of a session.

Follow-Ups

Marco Ball-O

Variations

Add a second team of players in the role of sharks for a competitive version of this game. In this version, the survivors have only 20 seconds to climb onto the life raft before the sharks are released from the edge of the pool. Sharks may munch on any survivors that are still in the water. A shark tagging a survivor instantly turns that survivor into a fellow shark. At the end of each two-minute round, declare that all remaining players who are not sharks are now survivors.

Teaching Tips

This is a good problem-solving game. Give players time to test out different strategies to see which method saves the greatest amount of survivors.

Humongous Water Foosball

Have you ever wondered what it would feel like to be one of those little plastic foosball players? We imagine that the satisfaction of being an integral part of such a cohesive team might be tempered by being forced to hang suspended from a steel rod. In any event, you and your players will get a sense of that experience in this soggy version of foosball. Participants should play this game in the shallow end of the pool.

Two teams form lines of players alternately facing each other, so they are in the same formation as the players on the rods of a foosball game. No two adjacent lines should feature players from the same team. The number of lines will depend on the size of your pool and how many players you have. Players should stand a bit more than two arm's lengths away from each other. You'll need at least two referees to launch the ball into the center of the court.

Objective

Teammates score one point by passing the big activity ball to the wall of the opponents' side of the pool. The team with the most points at the end of the game wins.

Additional Equipment

None

Safety Tips

Standard pool safety rules apply.

Lead-Ins

- Water Bomber
- Life Raft

Developmental Skills

- Primary skills include self-control and cooperation.
- Secondary skills include communication.

Duration of Game

The duration of the game depends on your group of players. Matches can last between several minutes and the duration of the session.

When to Play

This game can be the focus of a single play session. After warming up with a round of Swim-Overs or Swim-Unders, players will be ready.

Follow-Ups

- Ships Ahoy
- Octopus

Variations

Players may swim or wade away from their posts for a brief period of time. A nice way to set a time limit for these breaks is for players to use the one-breath rule. Players who move from the home position must repeatedly say something aloud. Players must return to home position before they take a second breath.

Teaching Tips

You can set limits for how far individual players can move from their initial positions.

Ships Ahoy

Ask any admiral, captain, first mate, ensign, or cabin boy what a ship needs to run smoothly and the answer will invariably be discipline. Ships Ahoy is a great game for finding out which team is the best at following orders. The game also reveals which captain has the best sea legs. The object of the game is for the captain to help the members of the crew, who have their eyes closed, navigate the treacherous waters ahead by calling out navigation signals.

A team consists of at least three mates who swim or wade around the ball with their eyes closed, and the captain, who sits on, lies on, or straddles the top of the ball. The crew tries to navigate the ball safely along the course as the captain calls out signals.

No progress can be made if the captain slides or falls off of the ball. A good rule of thumb for this game is actually the rule of shoulders. If either of the captain's shoulders touches the water, the team must stop and reposition the captain on top of the ball.

Objective

Players work cooperatively to keep their captain on top of the big activity ball. They also guide both the captain and the big activity ball across the pool while keeping their eyes closed.

Additional Equipment

An extra activity ball allows for direct, head-to-head competition. If you have only one ball, teams can compete against the clock.

Safety Tips

The course should be fairly far away from the sides of the pool so that the environment is safe if the captain accidentally slides off the ball.

Lead-Ins

Life Raft

Developmental Skills

- Primary skills include cooperation and communication.
- Secondary skills include trust.

Duration of Game

The course should be short enough so that teams can navigate one stretch in a few minutes.

When to Play

This game is appropriate at any time.

Follow-Ups

Water Bomber

Variations

You can introduce human buoys into the ocean for the ships to navigate around. Human buoys are other players who tread water in one location and regularly announce their presence with appropriate fog horn sounds. Another version of the game is played without a captain. The sailors still close their eyes as they navigate the ship through the course. They must now rely on the fog-horn sounds of the human buoys for directions.

Teaching Tips

It's okay if the sailors need to open their eyes once in a while. Ships Ahoy can be just as fun with wide-eyed pushers as it is with visually limited ones.

Octopus

The buoyant ropes used to create lanes for lap swimming define the sea lane in this game. A normal sea lane is about five or six times as wide as the ball. If you have lots of players, you can make the lane wider.

One player acts as the head of the octopus and sits on top of the ball. Three other players act as the tentacles of the octopus. The three tentacle players must always keep at least one hand on the ball. Two schools of fish line up on opposite edges of the pool. When the octopus gives the signal, all of the fish must swim to the opposite side of the pool, while staying in the lane. Fish who get tagged by an octopus tentacle attach themselves to the tentacle. As you can imagine, the octopus grows very quickly.

Players who swim to the other side of the pool without being tagged remain fish for the next round. At the next signal, the fish must swim across the pool again.

The game ends when only one fish remains, trying to elude the biggest octopus in the world.

Objective

The goal of the octopus players is to tag the fish as they cross from one side of the pool to the other. The goal of the fish players is to cross to the other side of the pool without being tagged by the octopus.

Additional Equipment

None

Safety Tips

Play the game in the shallow end of the pool unless all of the players are strong swimmers.

Lead-Ins

Water Bomber

Developmental Skills

- Primary skills include coordination.
- Secondary skills include cooperation.

Duration of Game

Each round usually lasts less than one minute.

When to Play

This game works well at the beginning, middle, or end of the session.

Follow-Ups

Life Raft

Variations

A headless octopus can still be quite a menace to sea life. Eliminate the player on top of the ball, and begin the game with three tentacle players touching the ball. In this variation, the tentacles must communicate with each other to decide which fish to pursue. Tentacles can only capture fish when they are attached to the head of the octopus.

Teaching Tips

The width of the lane greatly influences how easy it is for the octopus to tag fish. A narrower lane makes it easier for the octopus and a wider lane makes it easier for the fish.

You'll find other outstanding recreation resources at
www.HumanKinetics.com

In the U.S. call 1.800.747.4457
Australia 08 8372 0999
Canada. 1.800.465.7301
Europe . . . . .+44 (0) 113 255 5665
New Zealand 0800 222 062

HUMAN KINETICS
The Information Leader in Physical Activity
P.O. Box 5076 • Champaign, IL 61825-5076

About the Authors

Todd Strong, MSc, MEd, is an instructor for Surrey College in British Columbia, where he teaches courses in play, activity planning, and child development. As program director and lead trainer for the New Games Foundation, he has traveled throughout North America conducting play sessions and workshops and collecting and trying out hundreds of games in a variety of settings with many types of playgroups.

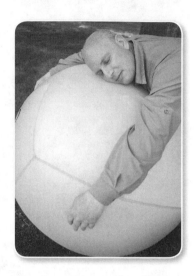

Strong was the lead author for *Parachute Games With DVD,* published by Human Kinetics, and he has also authored several instructional books on object-manipulation activities and on juggling (he is a columnist for *Juggle* magazine). He enjoys juggling, music, and bicycling in his spare time.

Bernie DeKoven, MA, has been active for 40 years in bringing innovation to recreation. He is the author of multiple books, including *Junkyard Sports* (Human Kinetics, 2005), which demonstrates innovative practices in creative play. He codirected the New Games Foundation, where he and others created numerous games to be played with an earth ball—a six-foot-diameter ball. DeKoven has a lifetime membership in the Association for Study and Play. In 2006 he received the Iffny-Reynolds Award from the North American Simulation and Gaming Society for outstanding work in the field of fun. His work blends with his play: He spends his leisure time inventing new games, modifying old games, and teaching people how to have more fun.